Art, Pottery, and the Clay-Human Connection

Understanding the Prophet Whom God Has Set in the Church!

> And God hath set some in the church, first apostles, secondarily prophets, thirdly teachers, after that miracles, then gifts of healings, helps, governments, diversities of tongues.
>
> —1 Corinthians 12:28 KJV

> Thus speaketh the Lord God of Israel, saying, Write thee all the words that I have spoken unto thee in a book.
>
> —Jeremiah 30:2 KJV

Dr. Alvin Haywood, Ed.D.

ISBN 979-8-88540-347-4 (paperback)
ISBN 979-8-88685-074-1 (hardcover)
ISBN 979-8-88540-348-1 (digital)

Copyright © 2022 by Dr. Alvin Haywood, Ed.D.

All rights reserved. No part of this publication may be reproduced, distributed, or transmitted in any form or by any means, including photocopying, recording, or other electronic or mechanical methods without the prior written permission of the publisher. For permission requests, solicit the publisher via the address below.

Christian Faith Publishing
832 Park Avenue
Meadville, PA 16335
www.christianfaithpublishing.com

All photos of the author are compliments of and used with permission from Steven Cotton Photography.

All other photos are used with permission through proof of license from Dreamstime, LLC photography provider.

Printed in the United States of America

Dr. Alvin Haywood Education and Prophetic Ministries

Making a positive impact on lives around the world one published book at a time on amazon.com

Messages of hope, healing, life, academic success, and new beginnings!

And I thank Christ Jesus our Lord, who hath enabled me, for that he counted me faithful, putting me into the ministry.

—1 Timothy 1:12

From the sick room, to the prayer room, to the Press Room!

I thank God for starting this Education & Prophetic Ministry and keeping it going, saying, "Now go, write it before them in a table, and note it in a book, that it may be for the time to come for ever and ever."

—Isaiah 30:8

Being confident of this very thing, that he which hath begun a good work in you will perform it until the day of Jesus Christ.

—Philippians 1:6

May you be blessed, be enlightened, and learn something new as you continue reading my book…

Contents

Introduction vii

Chapter 1: General Benefits of Participation in the Art of Pottery ... 1
                Benefits of school and community programs 1
                Focus and concentration 3
                Personal fulfillment 4
                The good mix between clay and music 4
                Sample music archaeology find 5
                Pottery as a hobby 5
                Pottery as a career 7
Chapter 2: Children Benefit from Working with Clay 11
                The physical-educational connection 12
                Social-emotional benefits of working with clay 14
                Building science concepts through work
                with modeling clay 14
                Some history lessons from clay pottery 16
Chapter 3: A Biblical Perspective on Walking in a
                Prophetic Calling 20
                Perspective defined and explained 20
                The influence of perspective on reading 21
                Never alone, ongoing direction, and
                wonderfully made 26
                Biblical cosmology 29
Chapter 4: Exploring the Example of Jeremiah the Prophet 37
                Called and equipped to be a prophet 38
                Spiritual "lockdown" 41

	Rejection of the prophet 54

               Rejection of the prophet 54
               God backs up the prophet..60
               One of Jeremiah's messages 61
               God validates his word through miracles,
               signs, and wonders! 62
Chapter 5:   A New Kind of 3 Rs: Release, Restoration, Revival...66
               Traditional methods of teaching.............................66
               Clay art studio learning..67
               Twenty-first century learning 69
               Release 73
               Restoration 75
               Revival 78
Chapter 6:   Conclusion..84

References 93

Introduction

Broadly speaking, art and creating works of art is the exploration of the cultural, spiritual, social, economic, and/or political aspects of the human experience. More specifically, art is the created imaginative and technical works of art, like the visual arts of painting and pottery (McIntosh 2017). Under the umbrella of the broad spectrum of art, works of pottery are vessels, or containers, that are made out of clay. The word "pot" refers to a vessel in the form of a container. One who is a potter usually refers to an individual artist who works in a studio, resulting in the term "studio pottery." A piece of clay is formed into a unique and personalized vessel on a potter's wheel where it is placed to be *molded* and *shaped* by the creative hands of the potter (Peterson 2019, p. 2). Potters take pride in their finished product.

The focus and *theme* of this book, the clay-human connection, takes that very concept—the pot in the hands of the potter—and compares it to a believer in the hands of God to be molded and shaped by him for their calling, especially a prophetic calling and especially those who happen to be single or unmarried as they walk in God's calling for them. The prophet, Jeremiah, was a prime example of God's perspective on walking in a victorious prophetic calling.

> But now, O Lord, thou art our father; we are the clay, and thou our potter; and we are the work of thy hand. (Isaiah 64:8 KJV)

In this book, scriptural references are taken from the King James Version of the Bible and labeled KJV or from the New International Version of the Bible and labeled NIV unless otherwise stated. Be blessed, and I hope that you will enjoy your continued reading of my book.

Original, natural clay is formed in the ground near the surface of the earth. It is soft and rich in substances from the earth. The formation of clay is a direct result of the erosion of rock due to weathering conditions. Because of the plasticity and flexibility of clay, it can be molded and shaped into an unlimited number of forms and shapes by human hands. Natural clay comes in an array of colors, depending on the chemical makeup of the soil in which it is found. For example, the kind of clay that is called *red clay* gets its red-orange or rusty-brownish color from iron oxide in the soil. Red clay can also be a color that looks like a blended mixture of tan and dark brown (Manoharan, Sutharsan, Dhanpandian, and Venkatachalapathy 2012; Minnesota Historical Society; Schmandt-Besserat 1977; Vasu 2011). Thus, red clay is not necessarily red.

Ancient pottery making, using clay, started sometime around 14,000 BC. Pottery was originally made and used for storing food and grains. People also used pottery as a way of showing their social identity or as a way to show the groups in which they were affiliated. Beautiful designs from some of the fabrics of their clothing were painted onto their pottery to show their family, society, and other group affiliations (Carr 2019). To put some context to the above 14,000 BC time period, when pottery making started, ancient clay tablets started being used for writing many years later around 3500 to 3200 BC. This writing started in the ancient civilization of Mesopotamia, which is now the country of Iraq in the Middle East. Mesopotamia was home to some ancient civilizations, such as the Sumerians, the Assyrians, and the Babylonians. Called cuneiform writing, the clay was dampened with water to allow for writing on it with a reed, a sharp instrument that was called a stylus. The cuneiform symbols were carved into the dampened clay. The early cuneiform writing that was started in ancient Mesopotamia was later replaced by alphabetic writing. The Egyptian writing system, called hieroglyphics, came into existence sometime before 3150 BC in Africa during the same time period of the start of the cuneiform writing in Mesopotamia. Egyptian hieroglyphic texts were closely connected to Egyptian artistic scenes (Archaeological Institute of America 2016; Capella 2008; Freeman-Ellis 1989; Mark 2011; Spencer 2003; Uchida and Watanabe 2014).

Archaeology is the study of the cultures and ways of life of ancient civilizations, including the artifacts, ceramics, and other objects that the people had made. Ceramics, which is one of the dimensions of archaeology, is key to understanding the development of ancient cultures and civilizations. Ceramics is what you get as a result of forming and shaping a piece of clay into a desired object and then firing it in a kiln. More specifically, to create beautiful ceramics or clay artwork, clay is mixed with water, and then the clay is shaped into a pottery container. The container can be a pot, jar, bowl, vase, or any other object formed from the clay. The pottery container is then fired, or baked in a large oven, called a kiln. Firing the clay at a very high temperature in the kiln gives stability and permanent structure to the clay container that was formed and shaped by the hands of the potter. After baking in the kiln, the hardened ceramic container can be painted in a single color or in multiple colors by the potter or by another person. The first brilliantly colored and beautiful glazes came into being when clay was mixed with other minerals and then fired in a kiln (Boehm, Hoone, McGowan, McKinney-Browning, Miramontes, and Porter 2000; Carr 2019; Friedel 2010; Griffiths 1999; Ion, Fierascu, Teodorescu, Turcanu-Cqrutiu, and Ion 2016; Violatti 2014; Woodford 2019). In addition to the study of ancient human cultures, archaeology also includes the study of ancient animal and plant specimens (Sawchuk and Prendergast 2019). Additionally, the scientific field of archaeology is concerned about and interested in reaching out to connect with the larger community for educational purposes and for community inclusion and collaboration (Brighton 2011).

Clay continues to be one of the most important minerals used for industry and for household needs, such as creating vessels for cooking and storage of food. Natural clay is also used for a variety of other purposes. Manufacturing of a variety of ceramic products is also important, like jewelry, floor tiles, and other materials for home-roofing installation or repair.

Over a third of all houses worldwide are made of clay. One-third of people in the world live in houses, or worship in churches or synagogues, that are made from clay that is mixed with organic materials. Called earthen architecture, these kinds of structures are good for increasing natural thermal insulation and for decreasing environmental pollution. Sun-dried clay housing structures are sustainable and cost-efficient because clay is a low-energy building material. Thus, pottery is critically important to the archaeologist's work, and clay is a vital material of life for sustenance in the home, for building and construction, for industrial matters, and for creating art by both children and adults (Bartel 2006; Breuer 2012; Djamil 2016; Friedel 2010; Mana, Hanafiah, and Chowdhury 2017; Manoharan et al. 2012; Peacock 1970; Stauback 2013).

As stated above, making pottery from clay and other natural materials has been an ongoing and critical component of human culture from way back in ancient and biblical times (Tsetlin 2018). The Bible uses the art of pottery to show how clay, in the hands of the potter, is similar to man in the hands of God (James 1962). Again, this clay-human symbolism is the *theme*—recurring thought or subject—of this book. This book will also explore and identify some of the trials and triumphs of those called into the office of a prophet of God. One of my favorite scriptures for encouragement in my calling is this one from the book of Isaiah:

> The Lord God hath given me the tongue of the learned, that I should know how to speak a word in season to him that is weary: he wakeneth morning by morning, he wakeneth mine ear to hear as the learned. (Isaiah 50:4 KJV)

One applicable story of a potter, and a prophet who was sent by God, is captured in the following passage of scripture that sets the stage for this book's clay-human connection theme. When you go where God tells you to go, there is a blessing waiting for you upon your arrival.

> The word which came to Jeremiah from the Lord, saying, Arise, and go down to the potter's house, and there I will cause thee to hear my words. (Jeremiah 18:1–2 KJV)

Hold these first two verses of scriptures in your mind. In chapter 3, these first two verses from the eighteenth chapter of the book of Jeremiah will be brought up again, reviewed, and then connected to Jeremiah 18:3–6. These scriptures provide vivid imagery of what Jeremiah the prophet saw and heard as God revealed to him the clay-human connection when Jeremiah obeyed the voice and leading of the Lord and went down to the potter's house. God sent him. It's always a great feeling when you know, without a doubt, that God has called and sent you!

Archaeologists study the cultures, or ways of life, of ancient civilizations.

Team of archaeologists sorting out and putting pieces of pots together from their archaeological dig.

Ceramic plates, cups, and bowls are the result of firing handmade objects of clay in a kiln. Later the ceramic pieces can be painted with beautiful designs.

Chapter 1

General Benefits of Participation in the Art of Pottery

Having access to and involvement in art education is beneficial to those in both general and special education programs. Integrating the arts into education and the curriculum gives meaning to learning experiences through authentic activities that are exploratory and self-directed. The arts also give adults and children a broader view of the world that helps develop new insights and understanding about events going on around them. Participation in the arts—including pottery, sculpture, architecture, music, and theater—promotes flexibility and independence and has a positive impact on social and academic achievement (Lloyd 2017).

Clay work is a *process* that involves manipulating and shaping clay and the clay *products* that result from engaging in clay activities. The successful completion of both the process and the product are important achievement outcomes for the artist. Since clay is known to be a natural material that is extracted from the earth, working with clay enriches the concept that clay work provides a human-earth connection (Sholt and Gavron 2006, p. 66).

Benefits of school and community programs

There are benefits to participants of all ages who engage in a pottery-making class or program. In addition to the critical importance of creative arts programs in the schools, those programs sponsored by the community are also particularly beneficial. Community-based classes and programs play a role in communication by providing a platform for participants to make friends, experience increased happiness, and interact with other participants across age, education, socioeconomic, career, and ability levels, including those with chronic illnesses. Participants can be voluntarily and actively involved with an activity that is of interest to them. These creative, mind-body interactive, collective, expressive, and interpersonal arts experiences help to build community and promote an overall sense of physical, mental, and social well-being (Genoe and Liechty 2017; Lusebrink 2004; Skibo and Feinman, 1999; Vellet 2014). Some people feel that just being around creative people and interacting with them in a productive and expressive art setting makes them feel creative.

In a study and investigation of a north-central valley of Honduras in ancient Central America, Joyce, Hendon, and Lopiparo (2014) concluded that learning a craft was tantamount to learning how to be a productive member of a social group. Clay work and other arts and crafts activities took place in both community gathering centers and in households nearby. These communal gathering places, or "communities of practice," provided opportunities for developing and strengthening social relationships among a diverse group of crafters. The craft and clay workers were bound together by their different levels of craft skills from various households. They were also linked together by the sharing of craft tools, and other resources, and working together to create pottery and ceramic products that enabled them to carry out their daily household and communal chores. This contributed to the making of their history and to their social, economic, political, and community development (Joyce et al. 2014, p. 411).

Regarding the benefits of community arts programs and art therapy for treating adult depression disorders, treating mental illness is best treated in a community setting, as opposed to in-house hospital programs. Hospital programs can be very expensive. In addition to taking one's regularly prescribed medication and other forms of treatment, art therapy in a community-based program is more cost effective than those in a hospital or health-care facility setting and can result in more positive emotional, physical, and other healthy outcomes.

Some community arts therapy programs are connected to university research programs. Graduate students can participate in service learning as they navigate designated coursework in a community setting through these university community center partnerships. This collaborative effort between a university and the community promotes community building and strengthens both the community and the student art therapy practitioners who provide services in those community-based centers (Feen-Calligan Moreno and Buzzard 2018).

Pottery is therapeutic and can be a stress reliever for older adults who may be experiencing mental-health concerns. Working with clay in a diverse community of family, friends, and others is beneficial for nourishing, stimulating, and strengthening both mind and body processes. Depression, fear, and anger can be lessened or entirely eliminated through meaningful interaction with clay, building human relationships, and creating personal pieces of clay work that are valuable to the participant (Genoe and Liechty 2017; Nan and Ho 2017).

Focus and concentration

Participation in the art of pottery gives one an outlet for focusing on their ambitions and personal-goal aspirations. Their stress level is reduced, thereby allowing them to be better able to concentrate solely on the pottery project at hand. There is also a boost in the self-confidence and self-esteem of participants who take pride in belonging to a community of other craft and pottery artists (Health Fitness Revolution 2019).

Otto (2016) reported on a study that showed that being involved in just a forty-five-minute art activity in an art therapy studio was sufficient enough to improve the participants' *self-efficacy*.

Having a sense of self-efficacy means that a person has the self-confidence to believe that they can complete a given task successfully. The participants in the study, who ranged in ages from eighteen to fifty-nine, used modeling clay and other art materials to create whatever they wanted. The study also showed that the art-making activity also resulted in positive feelings and an improvement in the mood of the participants. Other factors that probably contributed to these positive study results is that the activity took place in a supportive and nonjudgmental environment where there was no pressure to compete with others or perform at a preset performance standard.

Personal fulfillment

Creating something with clay provides participants with an interactive process that blends individual skill and imagination and results in personal fulfillment (Bae and Kim 2018). Through the lens of the potter, these participants value having a means whereby they can build their strength and motor skills as they produce a valued object by hand with clay in an intentional, personalized, and purposeful way. Engaging in leisure arts pottery activities also provides a venue for expressing one's talent in the arts, exploring and acting on your creative imagination, and experiencing personal, cognitive, social, and emotional growth and fulfillment. This motivation, in the context of positive purposes, leads to "an emotional involvement with the clay" (Brinck and Reddy 2019, p. 1; Genoe and Liechty 2017; Lloyd 2017). Having purpose and passion will spark creative motivation from the heart!

The good mix between clay and music

For over thirty-five thousand years, people have been making musical instruments out of a variety of materials, including stone, metal, wood, and pottery (Clark, Heflin, Kluball, and Kramer 2015). Some scholars believe that in some ancient civilizations, some of the first musical instruments, like drums, were made from clay pots that had been used for cooking (Westrup and Grame 2019). In his book, *From Mud to Music,* the author described how clay artists can make a variety of ceramic musical instruments. After reviewing ancient musical instruments from prehistoric times, artists can make replicas of these instruments. These clay-ceramic instruments can replicate prehistoric versions, or they can be made to resemble modern and more contemporary instrumental versions (Hall 2006).

Sample music archaeology find

One of the oldest musical instruments that can be found in most cultures is the rattle. Often decorated with symbols or designs, rattles were used to celebrate *new beginnings* of some kind. Small formations of hardened clay, or other beaded materials, were put into the rattle to give the rattle its noise-making capability (West 2018).

A North American prehistoric ceramic rattle was found by archaeologists in the 1950s in an area of the southwestern shoreline of the ancient Lake Cahuilla in Imperial County, California. The clay-ceramic rattle was intact and complete. It was used by North American Indians to accompany their singing and dancing at their festivals and celebrations. The rattles were probably also used as toys for children. The age of the rattle was estimated to date back to sometime between AD 950 and 1700. The rattle appeared to have been fired in an open pit kiln (Fenenga, Erwin, and Erwin 2015). Ceramic seriation is one of the scientific methods that archaeologists use for sequencing artifacts by date to assess and determine which ones were, chronologically, from earlier periods of time than others (Hirst 2018; LeCount 2018).

Pottery as a hobby

Pottery and ceramics are coming back as a hobby for those who have a passion and love for this creative art and want periods of productive break time from the increasing predominance of our technological society. Pottery provides a wholesome and soothing outlet that stimulates the mind, body, and soul while connecting the hobbyist to the historical significance of the importance of clay and ceramics to ancient cooking, homemaking, and farming practices. Pottery making gives the artist a block of creative time for critical thinking, meditation, an increased ability to relax, an improved and heightened state of mind or mood, and a deeper understanding of how pottery is intertwined with people, history, and culture (Genoe and Liechty 2017; Kimport and Robbins 2012; Skibo and Feinman 1999).

Some people are turning their hobbies into their own pottery studios or businesses at home or in their local business district (Godwin 2019). One way to view this transition is through the lens of a Christian or biblical perspective. Drawing thoughts from the title of chapter 3 of this book *A Biblical Perspective on Walking in a Prophetic Calling*, some years ago while walking in my prophetic calling (2007), I was led to turn my passion for teaching into my own home-based reading/language clinic (Haywood 2021). I had no idea that I would later become an author. Now, as a published author and continuing to walk in my calling, *my own books* are among many on display in that clinic, which now serves as a resource area and for mentoring. The real benefit of one's passion and creativity is to be able to connect them to the real world.

> And let the beauty of the Lord our God be upon us: and establish thou the work of our hands upon us: yea, the work of our hands establish thou it. (Psalm 90:17 KJV)

DiNardi (2019) postulated that engaging in and spending more time on your hobby can actually cause you to be more productive on your regular job. Like a musician or an artist singing or playing a song, the creativity of the potter causes him or her to think about how someone else might receive their carefully made and inspirationally produced piece of music, pot, or flower vase. Creativity and thoughtfulness about the feelings, perspectives, and well-being of others are critical interpersonal or people skills that are needed in today's rapidly changing and increasingly technological school classroom and workplace environments.

Pottery as a career

If you are studying art history, your course of study should be more than just teacher-centered lectures on the formal aspects of historical works of art. There is a move to make art history courses more student centered with technology being used as a tool for inquiry-based learning about the visual dimensions of art. Students are actively involved in constructing meaning for works of art. Multiple perspectives and interpretations of past and present art cultures are encouraged and explored in the context of a collaborative study of art and dialogue about people across a variety of languages and cultures (Martikainen 2017).

For expanding a pottery ceramics hobby into a full-time career, creating an online store presence on the internet gives you the opportunity to sell your creative products directly to your customers. The advantage of this internet strategy is that you can build your customer base from a worldwide pool of prospective buyers. Reaching out to art galleries to sell your pottery and participating in craft shows also will boost your marketing clientele. These various venues for marketing provide opportunities for your sharing, giving, and continued learning.

Axelsen and Arcodia (2004) reported on how art galleries and museums have taken on new directions that extend the art museum experience to much more than just walking through a gallery, looking at works of art on display. There has been an effort to make art galleries and museums more relevant to a broad range of diverse cultures, experiences, and interests. Visitors are encouraged to become actively involved with designated exhibits in some way through special events, such as workshops, engagement with a variety of art forms, musical presentations, and author book signings. The focus of art museums and galleries should be on educational purposes that increase motivation, participation, learning, fun, and enjoyment. Sawchuk and Prendergast (2019) described archaeology as the telling of the human story, which should include the equitable and collective voices of a cross section of community.

If you like to write and share what you are doing, starting a blog is also a good investment for promoting your work and letting others know what you do and how good you are at creating your works of art. Having an online presence provides a platform for sharing resources, and your presence puts you into the company of others interested in pottery and ceramics, thereby increasing and strengthening the arts community. Being flexible and open-minded are valuable assets for maintaining success in your pottery career (Fayt 2020).

The American Art Pottery Association (AAPA) and the American Ceramics Society (ACerS) are two member organizations that provide and promote educational resources for accessing materials and building knowledge and understanding of pottery and ceramics (Carringan 2019). Regarding pottery and creative arts lovers, the *Journal of the American Art Pottery Association* provides AAPA members with its quarterly publications four times a year. This journal contains beautiful photos of historical and contemporary works of pottery and research articles on potters and various topics on pottery. There is also valuable information about buying and selling creative pottery items. The AAPA has an annual convention that includes a two-day pottery show and auction sale of top-notch pottery items and ceramics.

Pottery and working with clay are creative art experiences enjoyed by both men and women. Women have a long history of continued success in creating clay pottery and ceramics for a variety of household functions and for decorative purposes. In the field of professional pottery, women have made great strides and accomplishments as pottery instructors, writers, business and gallery owners, and collectors of pottery and ceramic items (Vincentelli 2000). M. Louise Baker had a different kind of career in pottery. Her career involved the reproduction of archaeological artifacts. She was a highly acclaimed painter of Maya pottery and ceramics. The Mayans were also known for pyramids they built along the Yucatan Peninsula. The Yucatan is a peninsula in Southeastern Mexico that extends into the Gulf of Mexico. The Maya people were one of the ancient civilizations of the Americas that covered the area from central Mexico to northern Honduras in Central America. Ms. Baker's paintings of Mayan pottery are so amazingly impressive that "one can almost feel the weight of the clay, the depth of the incising, or the curve of the neck" (Capella 2008; Danien 2006, p. 4).

The ideal situation for interpreting primitive archaeological finds is for the archaeologist to, in addition to working with physical scientists, also include a professional craft artist on the research team, such as a pottery-ceramic art specialist. An expert in pottery and ceramics with some basic knowledge about archaeology can greatly add their insight to the establishment of data about a particular archaeological find. A professional skilled craft artisan can, through collaborative examination and thought, help the archaeologist determine what certain pottery finds may have meant in the daily lives of those ancient groups of people (Botwid 2013). Creative work, including work with clay, is a crucial link for improving and enhancing human development. Creative work allows people to interact with their passions. They also experience dignity and can turn their leisure interests into gainful employment (Kabanda 2015).

The Bible uses clay and the art of pottery to show the strong connection between clay being molded and shaped in the hands of a potter and man being formed, molded, and shaped in the hands of God.

Being involved with pottery gives one a practical appreciation of how pottery and ceramics are connected to history and diverse groups of people and their ways of life.

Chapter 2

Children Benefit from Working with Clay

Modeling clay is a valuable tool in the hands of children for engaging in constructive play. Constructive play sparks the imagination of young children, leading them to explore, create, and build objects of their choice. These hands-on and inquiry-based learning experiences are accompanied by lots of active questioning by children, personal interactions with their peers, and discovery of new ideas (Drew, Christie, Johnson, Meckley, and Neil 2008).

Working with clay speaks to the playful and spontaneous nature of children. Clay work and creating pottery may be classified as formal learning if it is part of an organized class or structured pottery/ceramics educational course or program. Creative pottery making can also be considered informal or experiential learning if it is learning in the context of one's daily life and/or leisure time activities. Both kinds of learning, formal and informal, fall under the umbrella of lifelong learning if you have a desire to continue to learn and build your skills in designated areas of interest throughout your life. Clay, because of its flexibility and how it is made, is a unique and valuable medium of art for exploring a wide variety of educational and personal fulfillment goals (Boudreau 1923; Laal and Salamati 2012; Vellet 2014).

Curriculum, in the context of lifelong learning, is the total of all planned learning experiences. These planned learning experiences take place throughout one's life, wherever the learning experiences may be. This is called lifelong learning, which spans an individual's formal and informal learning and leisure time activities, their work, and their life (Clark 2015).

As children, many of us can remember the joys of playing and working with clay at home, during art time at school, or in those community art classes at the local recreation center and/or the art museum. Just as clay is molded and shaped by the potter, children are *molded and shaped* by the adults in their lives and their life experiences. Regarding adjustment to early school experiences, parents can have a profound influence on the molding of their children in three critical ways: (1) having high expectations for their children that will enhance their school academic and social success, (2) providing early stimulation of reading and number/mathematics experiences for their children at home, and (3) maintaining parent-child interactions that are consistent and meaningful (Lunenburg 2011; Mustard 2010). Wong and Benson (2019) highlighted how meaningful talk with other children and adults during creative art processes develops the listening and comprehension skills of children and helps to prepare them for later formal reading development in the context of active participation in hands-on art experiences.

The physical-educational connection

Squeezing, pressing, rolling, pushing, pulling, and pounding on a piece of clay gives the fingers and hands a good physical workout. This robust exercising of the hands and fingers lends itself well to small and large muscle development and coordination of the eyes and hands. Physical development of these muscles is directly related to success in early writing skills, handling of books, engaging with technology, buttoning clothing, tying shoes, and many other fine and gross muscle skill competencies needed at home and at school. The open-ended and flexible nature of working with clay also fosters a child's imagination and critical thinking skills. Opportunities for communication with others around them is enhanced, as well as genuine hands-on learning, increased motivation, a sustained attention span, and an enhancement of independent creativity (Bartel 2006; Erickson 2015).

Creating with clay is a lot like creating while writing. In pottery making, you're playing with clay and remodeling the object being created as needed. In the writing class, you're creating a piece of writing by playing with words and revising your manuscript as needed. The key point of the comparison of these two activities—pottery and writing—is that true learning comes through taking risks, through the process of trial and error, perseverance, making mistakes, learning from those mistakes, moving forward, and never giving up (Carlo 2017).

Play-Doh, the familiar counterpart to modeling clay, is a commercial product that provides similar benefits for children. Like modeling clay, Play-Doh also helps to develop the small and large hand muscle functions and eye-hand coordination in young children as they squeeze, roll, flatten, and poke their Play-Doh. Their language and vocabulary skills are also being developed as children verbalize their excitement about what they are creating with their soft and colorful Play-Doh. Play-Doh also provides opportunities for young children to see patterns and practice early math skills and concepts by comparing and contrasting different shapes of Play-Doh and by using cookie cutters to cut out letters and numbers to create and solve simple math equations and problems (Mugurussa 2012; Ranson 2019; Swartz 2005).

Like Play-Doh, clay comes in a variety of colors; but the different colors of clay are natural. Clay comes in different colors, depending on the chemical and mineral makeup of the soil in which it was found. Paint stores use the pigment (color) of clay to add to their paint to get a variety of colors for home painting, etc. Children would enjoy a field trip to a paint store to see firsthand how the physical and chemical properties of clay allow it to distribute itself evenly throughout the paint base of paint in a paint can (Foley 2009; Manoharan et al. 2012).

Social-emotional benefits of working with clay

Being intensely involved with creating something from clay brings a sense of calm and quietness to children. Making mistakes with the formation of an intended clay object can be easily reshaped and fixed as many times as needed to reconfigure the work of clay in progress. Thus, children can work at their own pace without feeling pressured to come up to a premeasured standard of ability (Bandoim 2015).

Like creative play with blocks, plastic Lego blocks, and other exploratory learning activities, when working with clay in a pottery class or other group setting, children have opportunities to build both their cognitive and social-relationship skills with their peers and with adults. Sometimes, just playing with clay releases a lot of pent-up emotions. Pottery and clay activities promote language, vocabulary, and social-emotional development as children share, collaborate, and talk about what they are creating with their piece of clay. Children can see their thinking and learning emerge and progress along to a finished piece of clay artwork.

This clay work process helps to build bridges and *connect* children to an ancient form of art that was used thousands of years ago. Therefore, working with clay is a multidisciplinary, interactive, and holistic learning activity that enhances the child's overall physical, mental, educational, social, emotional, and creative artistic expression development (Bandoim 2015; Erickson 2015; Jang and Choi 2012; Nespeca 2012; Sussman 2012; Terreni 2015).

Building science concepts through work with modeling clay

Classified as one of the visual arts, along with drawing, painting, sculpture, photography, weaving, and other textile crafting arts, modeling and working with clay is amenable to integrating and developing science and engineering concepts. Working with clay builds children's skills needed for later advanced coursework and/or careers in science, technology, engineering, and math (STEM). Children have opportunities to engage in trial-and-error processes where taking risks, making mistakes, and persistence are all a part of learning. For example, students may engage in a clay activity that encourages small groups of children to form and shape the same amount of clay into a clay structure that will sink in water, as opposed to a clay structure that will float on the water (physical science). Through planning, collaboration, negotiation, scientific investigation, and testing their predictions about why their formations should sink, the ultimate learning goal is that children will discover that clay, shaped and formed into a ball, is more likely to sink.

In another activity, children use a balance scale with a certain amount of clay on one side of the scale. Small groups of children work together to determine how much clay they need to measure out for the container on the other side of the scale to make the scale balance. This activity also involves the development of collaborative, negotiation, and math-reasoning skills (Bustamante, Greenfield, and Nayfeld 2018; McIntosh 2017; Noice, Noice, and Kramer 2014).

Earth science, geology, and chemistry are involved when students study and discover and/or review that soil is formed from the weathering and erosion of rocks, due to rain and other seasonal conditions (earth science). Clay, in its natural form, is dug up out of the soil from beneath the surface of the earth (geology). Clay comes in a variety of natural colors due to the various kinds of chemical makeup (chemistry) of the soil in which it had been embedded in for long periods of time. Thus, clay is impacted by the weathering of rock and formation of the soil. If you want to dig up some clay yourself, clay can be found on the bank of streams at places where construction is going on and/or sometimes in your own backyard under the topsoil.

Kaolinite is the most prevalent of the five major minerals found in clay. Kaolinite, a soft white mineral, is often changed to a red or orange color by iron oxide in the soil, resulting in red and/or reddish-orange clay. Iron oxide is a mineral that is a mixture of iron and oxygen. In the United States, kaolinite is mostly found in the mountainous regions of North Carolina (Bartel 2006; Manoharan et al. 2012; Righi and Meunier 1995; Vasu 2011). Students can use a periodic table of elements (chemistry) to learn about symbols for various elements and observe that the chemical symbol for iron is *Fe*, and the chemical symbol for oxygen is *O* (Sharp 2017).

Some history lessons from clay pottery

Children and students of all ages can learn that pottery is the end result of having changed clay (a plastic material) into a ceramic object (or nonplastic material). Pottery is the most common artifact found on ancient archaeological sites (Nicholson 2009). People started making pottery, or containers made of clay, thousands and thousands of years ago. Archaeologists are the professionals who study the cultures or ways of life of ancient civilizations. At that time, many pottery vessels were made by just pushing a hole up into a ball of clay. Since clay is so amenable, flexible, and easy to mold and form into so many different things, clay is compared to and viewed as the plastic of ancient civilizations.

In ancient Sumer, the Sumerians were able to produce mass amounts of pottery items through the use of their turning pottery wheel. Sumer was in the southern part of ancient Mesopotamia, which is now the country of Iraq in the Middle East. It runs along the banks of the Euphrates and Tigris rivers. Being able to produce pottery items in mass quantities resulted in an economic and business venue that allowed the Sumerians to trade their items with other people. The Sumerians later began to write on dampened clay tablets to keep an inventory of the goods that they were creating and selling to people in and around the community.

People in Mesopotamia were making pottery long before they were farming, planting, and cultivating crops. When they did start farming. Their chief crop was barley. Mesopotamia was the first ancient civilization to make beer, which was fermented from barley bread. Their diet also included fruits and vegetables and meat from mostly goats, pigs, and sheep.

Children should also know that natural clay has a long history, among other antibacterial treatments, for treating and healing skin infections and other adverse skin conditions. Clay minerals, mixed with water, have also been used to form cosmetics or pastes and gels for protection and cleansing of the skin. These clay-water mixture skin treatments have been much less costly than the more high-end, pricey, commercial brands. Clay minerals also have a long history of being used in pharmaceutical mixtures and medicines to treat stomach problems and protect the lining of the intestines from bacteria and other harmful toxins (Boehm et al. 2000; Curretero 2002; Karim and Amin 2018; Kiger 2019; Mark 2014; Williams and Haydel 2010).

Pottery is classified as one of the arts-and-crafts activities that can be used in everyday living. Pottery is also used for creative and decorative arts purposes. Pottery can include any number of items, such as pots and containers for cooking, vessels for pouring liquids, jugs, and an array of beautiful dishes (Martin, Obille, Apigo, Gongora, Labsan, Navalta, and Oringo 2016). Just like modern-day dishes and cookware, ancient pottery finds have to be cleaned too. Once it has been excavated or dug up from the earth, it must be carefully and methodically cleaned to make sure that it doesn't lose any of its original features. For valid restoration of the object, choosing the safest strategy for cleaning the artifact is of utmost importance. Pottery fragments and pots excavated from under the earth's surface can be covered with various kinds of dirt, dust, particles of soil, and other kinds of materials. While cleaning, extreme care must be taken by the archaeologist or the cleaning conservator, not to damage or destroy any original features of the artifact or the pottery object (Abd-Allah, al-Muheisen, and al-Howad 2010).

Whether in Asia, Africa, Europe, or in North, Central, or South America, one of the many purposes for making clay pots and jars was to store and preserve fish and/or grains. Fish was stored to later make fish sauce. A good primary grade children's book that can be read aloud to children, or one that they can independently read and explore, is titled *A Is for the Americas* by Cynthia Chin-Lee and Terri de la Peña (1999). This is a colorful alphabet book that, using the twenty-six letters of the alphabet, eloquently describes the rich cultural heritage, language, customs, food, and natural geography of the people of North, Central, and South America. The pictures are large and colorful in this larger ten-by-ten-and-a-half hardcover book. The English, Spanish, and French languages are highlighted in this book about the Americas, also called the New World, since it is younger than Africa, Asia, and Europe. Another children's book on ancient history to take a look at is *Ancient History: Explore the Past* (Capella 2008; Chin-Lee, and de la Peña 1999).

The making of pottery continued to spread all over the world. Later on, people began to use a wooden potter's wheel to help shape, mold, and build their pots as the piece of clay was pressed, pinched, pounded, and controlled by the expert and creative hands of the potter. The pottery wheel allowed the potter to make their pots and other items a lot faster. A wooden platform was spun on an axle by being kicked and pushed by the potter, as the lump of clay gradually changed and evolved into a desired vessel and work of art (Carr 2017; Tite 2008).

Pottery wheels are still used today in modern society. A potter's wheel can be the type that are operated by the potter kicking his or her leg against a kick wheel, or there are now electronic pottery wheels. A small electric pottery wheel can be used to form and make smaller clay objects, but a larger electronic high-powered potter's wheel is needed for making very large pots and other large objects out of clay. However, the greatest tool for the potter is their *hands* (Humphries 2017). I love the song "Hold to God's Unchanging Hand" (Marovich 2012).

This brings us back to the Bible story of the potter in Jeremiah 18:1–2 where these first two of six verses were given in the introduction section. All six relevant scriptures, Jeremiah 18:1–6, are stated later in the fifth paragraph of chapter 3. The Bible uses parables, illustrations, short stories, or live events of naturally occurring agricultural, cultural, and/or other human experiences to bring spiritual enlightenment and understanding of a spiritual concept or lesson.

ART, POTTERY, AND THE CLAY-HUMAN CONNECTION

Elementary school-aged children giving their hands a thorough and creative workout in the art clay studio.

Science teacher teaching a unit on geology. Geology is the study of the physical characteristics of the earth, including rocks and the processes that impact the earth's materials.

Chapter 3

A Biblical Perspective on Walking in a Prophetic Calling

> Thus saith the Lord of hosts; Let your hands be strong, ye that hear in these days these words by the mouth of the prophets, which were in the day that the foundation of the house of the Lord of hosts was laid, that the temple might be built.
> —Zechariah 8:9 KJV

Perspective defined and explained

Perspective is a point of view that someone holds or their way of viewing a particular subject or idea. People will often say. "This is the way I see it." Ayee (2013) explained and elaborated on how our perspectives and ways of communicating are influenced and shaped by our belief system, attitude, and our lived experiences. Our lived experiences, in turn, have an impact on how we think, behave, and how we respond to the everyday situations of life. For example, my perspective on Bible scripture is that scripture is God, expressly speaking to all of mankind and to each of us personally. I can feel the voice, presence, and power of God whenever I meditate on the following passage of scripture:

> Thus saith the Lord, thy redeemer, and he that formed thee from the womb, I am the Lord that

maketh all things; that stretcheth forth the heavens alone; that spreadeth abroad the earth by myself. (Isaiah 44:24 KJV)

One of our early lived experiences that has a profound impact on our attitude and perspectives toward reading is if we were read to as a child. Regarding school readiness and early reading development, research has shown that reading aloud to children is one of the most important reading activities that positively impacts a child's listening comprehension and their readiness for school. Reading aloud also helps to develop positive attitudes toward reading and a love for reading. This leads to stable and ongoing lifelong reading habits (Lunenburg 2011; Short, Lynch-Brown, and Tomlinson 2014). For many, lifelong reading includes the Bible.

The influence of perspective on reading

In the teaching of academic reading, it is very important that students are able to comprehend or understand what they are reading. For constructing meaning of text, the reader-response theory (or transactional theory by Rosenblatt 1978) says that there must be an interconnected and mutual relationship between the text of the author and the reader. In other words, the reader's understanding of, connection to, and *perspective* on a given piece of written text will be influenced by his/her background knowledge of the subject of the text and the reader's personal experiences. The reader brings meaning to the text by being able to connect to and relate to what is being read.

This comprehension/reader response/perspective scenario will be true, whether you're reading in a school classroom setting or in a church Sunday school class. Multiple perspectives, understanding, and interpretations occur as the reader draws from their background knowledge and experiences. This enables the reader to come together with the written text that they are reading and discussing and apply it to his or her own life. For example, in a Sunday school class discussion, students get a good understanding of particular scriptures from the lesson when they can connect to it and see how particular scriptures relate to their lives. Class discussion is one of many valuable teaching strategies for encouraging active participation and student learning. If you've experienced healing in your body from a particular illness, your perspective, understanding, and response to a designated Bible scripture(s) may be different than others in the class who may have had different experiences in the context of that same text of scripture (Biggams and Itterly 2007; Bristol and Isaac 2009; Mark 2019; Sanders 2012).

Here is a set of scriptures that are an example of a God-inspired, prophetic, and biblical perspective of the ancient art of pottery that uses Jeremiah the prophet, observing a potter at the potter's wheel, forming, molding, shaping, and reshaping a piece of clay into a vessel:

> The word which came to Jeremiah from the Lord, saying, Arise, and go down to the potter's house, and there I will cause thee to hear my words.
>
> Then I went down to the potter's house, and behold, he wrought a work on the wheels. And the vessel that he made of clay was marred in the hand of the potter: so he made it again another vessel, as seemed good to the potter to make it.
>
> Then the word of the Lord came to me, saying, O house of Israel, cannot I do with you as this potter? Saith the Lord. Behold, as the clay is in the potter's hand, so are ye in mind hand, O house of Israel. Jeremiah 18:1–6 (KJV).

Here we see that this spiritual lesson takes place in three stages in verses 1–6:

Stage 1: Jeremiah is sent by God to a particular setting (the potter's house) to receive the lesson.

Stage 2: At the potter's house, or on this personally assigned field trip, Jeremiah observed and learned how the potter had complete *control* over the piece of clay in his hands to make it and revise it into what he wanted the piece of clay to be.

Stage 3: God (the great teacher) then interpreted and urged Jeremiah to reflect upon how, just like the clay is formed, molded, and shaped in the potter's hands, the people of God can be *formed, molded,* and *shaped* in the hands of God. Redoing and reshaping the piece of clay, after it had been marred, is a symbol of how God is able to work on his people and transform them into something new. Again, this is one of the main *themes* of this book: the clay-human connection.

The popular Christian spiritual song "Have Thine own way, Lord!" by Adelaide A. Pollard (1907) goes along with Jeremiah 18:3–6. This song gives praise to God for being the potter and then asks him to have his way with us as the clay. Since he made us, he knows all about us and will provide all of our needs (Hawn 2013). God compares his people to an array of beautiful jewelry and valuable pieces of pottery that are formed and shaped in the hands of the potter.

> And they shall be mine, saith the Lord of hosts, in that day when I make up *my jewels*; and I will spare them, as a man spareth his own son that serveth him. (Malachi 3:17 KJV)

> Though the precious people of Zion were like fine gold, how they are valued like the clay vessels, the handiwork of the potter. (Lamentations 4:2 International Standard Version ISV)

Cantrell (2001) reported that the potter at the potter's house in Jeremiah 18:3 was named Yonadav. As Jeremiah watched, Yonadav was rolling, squeezing, and pressing on the clay just as a bread maker kneads bread dough. Kneading bread dough means that moistened flour, just like clay, is rolled, squeezed, and pressed to make bread. Since we are talking about bread, Kourkouta, Koukourikos, Iliadis, Ouzounakis, Monios, and Tsaloglidou (2017) pointed out that bread is the basic staple of a balanced daily diet. Also, a spiritual connection to bread is highlighted in the book of John where Jesus proclaims a basic principle about himself:

> And Jesus said unto them, I am the bread of life: he that cometh to me shall never hunger; and he that believeth on me shall never thirst. (John 6:35 KJV)

The spiritual concepts and life's lessons, using imagery of a potter working with a piece of clay and reshaping it as needed, is also meant to be a description of a biblical perspective that shows God's feelings about his *relationship* with his people—*the church.*

> What? Know ye not that your body is the *temple* of the Holy Ghost, which is in you, which ye have of God, and that ye are not your own? (1 Corinthians 1:19 KJV)

> For we are labourers together with God: ye are God's husbandry, ye are God's building. (1 Corinthians 3:9 KJV)

With all of our mistakes, failures, and "beating ourselves up" about the many detrimental things that we may have done in the past, God is able to equip and qualify us and cause us to be useful, productive, successful, and honorable workers—*vessels*—for him (Ezrachimts 2016).

> They shall not build, and another inhabit; they shall not plant, and another eat: for as the days of a tree are the days of my people, and mine elect shall long enjoy the work of their hands. (Isaiah 65:22 KJV)

Even when someone has become a broken vessel, God is able to pick them up, brush them off, and then put them back together again. Richman-Abdou (2019) described a longtime historical Japanese method of art for repairing broken pottery called *kintsugi* or *kintsukuroi*. Instead of trying to hide the broken cracks with invisible adhesive, the pottery or ceramic pieces are joined back together with dusted gold or silver tree sap lacquer.

The idea behind this creative art process is that you don't always have to try to hide age, wear and tear, or scars. Sometimes you can't. Something that has been scarred or broken can be given another chance of being even more beautiful than before it was broken. This Japanese art concept can be seen time and time again with people who have been "broken" by one or more adverse or traumatic circumstances in their life, but they were able to show resilience in being able to adapt to and deal with the difficult event(s) and bounce back to a state of living, which was better than before they were "broken" (Dalile 2015; Richman-Abdou 2019).

The Bible story of Job is a good example of this *kintsugi* concept of how broken pottery, or anything or anybody, can be repaired to look or be even better than they did before they were broken. Job, through his severe illness, ongoing criticism from his so-called friends, and other trials and tribulations, held on to his faith and trust in God, declaring, "But he knoweth the way that I take: when he hath tried me, I shall come forth as gold" (Job 23:10 KJV).

Even though someone may have experienced illness, the loss of loved ones, being hurt, let down, overlooked, and/or rejected, no one has to stay hurt and broken. The people of God are like *clay* jars that might get broken. Like broken clay jars, the people of God can not only be put back together again and healed, but they can also be useful, instrumental, and resourceful in encouraging and inspiring others to believe and receive their own physical, emotional, and/or spiritual restoration and their overall miracles of healing from God (Im 2017).

> But we have this treasure in earthen *vessels,* that the excellency of the power may be of God, and not of us. (2 Corinthians 4:7 KJV)

Certain songs can be so uplifting! There is a song by Rich Mullins entitled "Awesome God." The first line of the song says, "Our God is an awesome God," and then the song goes on to proclaim and repeat that "he reins" (Mullins 1988). God can fix anything!

Like the transformation and change in the newly formed and molded piece of clay in the potter's hand, there comes a divine change and newness of life in people in the hands of God:

> Therefore if any man be in Christ Jesus, he is a new creature: old things are passed away; behold all things are become new. (2 Corinthians 5:17 KJV)

> And ye are *complete in him*, which is the head of all principality and power. (Colossians 2:10 KJV)

Regarding the above scripture from Colossians, no one in Christ Jesus, especially and including single parishioners, should be allowing anyone to imply or try to convince them that they are alone and "all by themselves" and/or incomplete when the Word of God tells them otherwise!

Never alone, ongoing direction, and wonderfully made

Furthermore, the children of God aren't just left there to fend for themselves, but there is a sure promise of follow up care and guidance. We are never alone as Jesus promised in many relevant and applicable scriptures, such as these two from the book of Psalms and the book of Matthew that say:

> I will instruct thee and teach thee in the way which thou shalt go: I will guide thee with mine eye. (Psalm 32:8 KJV)

> and, lo, I am with you always, even unto the end
> of the world. Amen. (Matthew 28:20)

God is always with a believer no matter the season, the situation, the hard times, the illness, time of life or whatever he or she may be going through and experiencing at any given time.

> And even to your old age I am he; and even to
> hoar [gray] hairs will I carry you: I have made,
> and I will bear; even I will carry and will deliver
> you. (Isaiah 46:4 KJV)

The above scripture, along with so many others, is a confirmation that God is not just concerned about those in their earlier years and young adult life, but he is equally concerned about those who are in their advanced years of life. In Exodus 3:2, 10, Moses was *eighty years old* when the angel of the Lord appeared to him in the burning bush and told him that he would be the one to lead Israel out of Egypt. This amazing event is also recorded in the New Testament:

> And when he [Moses] was full forty years old, it
> came into his heart to visit his brethren the children of Israel. And when forty years were expired,
> there appeared to him in the wilderness of Mount
> Sinai an angel of the Lord in a flame of fire in a
> bush. (Acts 7:23, 30 KJV)

Do not think, say, or let anybody else try to convince you that you are too old to be used by God. Remember that song that many of us sing, "Where He Leads Me, I Will Follow" written by Ernest W. Blandy (1890). This Christian gospel song was written from the perspective of the scripture from the book of Matthew: "Then said Jesus unto his disciples, If *any* man will come after me, let him deny himself, and take up his cross and follow me" (Matthew 16:24 KJV). In other words, when singing this song, you are saying that you are determined to not only go where God is leading you to go, but you are willing to give yourself to him in all areas of your life, regardless of your position or status in life. It is important to not only practice what you teach or preach, but it is also important to practice what you sing! There are no limitations, lines of separation, or age barriers in God. We are all in this together, for the scripture says:

> Then shall the virgin rejoice in the dance, *both young men and old together*: for I will turn their mourning into joy, and will comfort them, and make them rejoice from their sorrow. (Jeremiah 31:13 KJV)

In the field of genetics, science tells us that, except for identical twins, each of us has a unique DNA profile. DNA (deoxyribonucleic acid) is a chemical that is located inside the many cells that we have in our body. More specifically, each cell in our body has a nucleus, which is located in the center of each cell. Chromosomes are located inside each cell nucleus. Our DNA is inside of these chromosomes. Our DNA determines our identity and character traits. Our DNA also determines what each of us look like—our height, eye color, skin tone. Each person's fingerprints have a unique underlying skin pattern so that no two people have the same fingerprints (Briggs 2017; Lynch and Hancock 2012; O'Hagan and Calder 2020; Straiton 2018).

> I will praise thee; for I am fearfully and wonderfully made: marvelous are thy works; and that my soul knoweth right well. (Psalm 139:14 KJV)

Thus, each of us, indeed, are one of a kind and *wonderfully* made by God and made for a divine purpose. Do you know what your purpose or calling is in this life? Isn't it great when you know?

There are no second-class citizens with God that are based on age, race, gender, or marital status. Again, we are all in this together!

Therefore, no one should be treated unjustly, devalued, troubled, intimidated, or harassed in their sincere efforts to serve God based on any of those status categories. One of the feature scriptures that, clearly and distinctly, speaks to and provides a message for the harassers would be this one from the book of Thessalonians:

> And that ye study to be quiet, and to *do your own business*, and to work with your own hands, as we commanded you. (1 Thessalonians 4:11 KJV)

Taking care of our own business leaves no time for meddling with the affairs of others. The following couple of scriptures provide protection and comfort for those troubled by others:

> And will not God bring about justice for his chosen ones, who cry out to him day and night? Will he keep putting them off? I tell you, he will see that they get justice, and quickly… (Luke 18:7–8 NIV)

> but he that troubleth you shall bear his judgment, whosoever he be. I would they were even cut off which trouble you. (Galatians 5:10, 12 KJV)

Biblical cosmology

Broadly speaking, Roberts (2013) described how biblical cosmology consists of the heavens above and the earth under the heavens. The Christian biblical-theological view stresses that creation involved one God. The following three scriptures express an expansive view of the continued manifestation of the creative work of the *hands* of God:

> The heavens declare the glory of God; and the firmament sheweth his handywork. (Psalm 19:1

> KJV) (The word, firmament, is referring to the sprawling nature of the sky or the heavens.)

> Of old hast thou laid the foundation of the earth; and the Heavens are the work of thy hands. (Psalm 102:25 KJV)

> Before the mountains were born or you brought forth the whole world, from everlasting to everlasting you are God. (Psalm 90:2 NIV)

That the cosmos consisted of the heavens above and the earth below was also the belief of the ancient Mesopotamians. The difference between the Mesopotamian view and the biblical cosmology view was a theological one. A theological difference means a difference in theology or beliefs about the nature of God, religious principles, observances, and religious practices. The ancient Mayan civilization theological view promoted the idea that the cosmos was created by multiple images of beings, gods, or deities. The Maya built temples, which served as housing for the images of their gods, such as their sun god and the rain god. The first of these stone pyramid temples were built over two thousand years ago. Some of the temples could be as high as two hundred feet. The images of their gods could be found painted on their ancient ceramic pottery vessels (Boehm et al. 2000; Choi 2008; Garcia 2018; Houston 1999; Roberts 2013).

Joshua, who became the leader of the people of Israel right after Moses, gathered all the people together and made this strong, confident, and heartfelt proclamation to all of them:

> And if it seem evil unto you to serve the Lord, choose you this day whom ye will serve; whether the gods which your fathers served that were on the other side of the flood, or the gods of the Amorites, in whose land ye dwell: but as for me

and my house, we will serve the Lord. (Joshua 24:15 KJV)

If I ever think that I can't get through a particular problematic situation, God redirects my thinking by gently reminding me of his unlimited and all-encompassing power and asking me a question, "Behold, I am the Lord, the God of all flesh: is there any thing too hard for me?" (Jeremiah 32:27 KJV). This biblical truth is reaffirmed by Paul in his first letter to the Corinthians and in the book of Psalms:

> For the earth is the Lord's, and the fulness thereof. (1 Corinthians 10:26 KJV)

> Our help is in the name of the Lord, who made heaven and earth. (Psalm 124:8 KJV)

With God being the potter and creator of mankind, *the people of God* are spiritually spoken of and seen as *pottery* or vessels. God is the potter. Thank God, I am the pot in him, the Potter.

> For *in him* we live, and move, and have our being; as certain also of your poets have said, For we are also his offspring. (Acts 17:28 KJV)

It's a blessing to be able to get up and move!

> And that he might make known the riches of his glory on the *vessels* of mercy, which he had afore prepared unto glory. (Romans 9:23 KJV)

Peckham (2007) emphasized that God's sovereignty, or authority and control, is supreme over all things. This book's continued main *theme* is, like the potter is in control of the clay that is in his or her hands, God is in ultimate control of his people and all creation that are in his hands!

From a child, I have a picture in my mind and remember that song "He's Got the Whole World in His Hands." This African American spiritual song was first published in 1927 (Nelson 2005). God is still in control even though he gives us a measure of free will, whereby our actions and the choices we make will have an impact (good or bad) on our personal well-being, current events, and/or on the environment. Thus, Artson (2009) pointed out that we often end up playing a part in the shaping of our life events and the resulting outcomes.

> Be not deceived; God is not mocked: for whatsoever a man soweth, that shall he also reap. (Galatians 6:9 KJV)

Generally speaking, potters are skilled and talented people who make a variety of objects out of clay. Their hands are a special tool for turning simple pieces of clay into valuable, functional, and usable items—*applied art*. One of the challenges of being an effective potter is having and maintaining a stable and steady set of hands to manipulate and mold the piece of clay with which you are working. A potter must pay attention to detail if the desired structure and quality of the object is to be realized and accomplished. God, as the potter and creator of mankind, paid attention to detail when creating and forming mankind and continues to pay attention to detail as he shapes us, individually, into what he wants us to be and do in this life (Asbell and Head 2014; Elbrecht and Antcliff 2014; Mitchell 2018; Sutakova and Mestnikov 2018).

> Know ye that the Lord he is God: it is he that hath made us, and not we ourselves; we are his people, and the sheep of his pasture. (Psalm 100:3)

> The hearing ear, and the seeing eye, the Lord hath made even both of them. (Proverbs 20:12 KJV)

We must remember not to fight against God's will and his plan for us, and we should pray that God will help us to not let others lead us astray from his plan, no matter who they may be!

> Woe to those who quarrel with their Maker, those who are nothing but potsherds among the potsherds on the ground. Does the clay say to the potter, What are you making? Does your work say, The potter has no hands? (Isaiah 45:9 NIV)

In the above verse of scripture, a potsherd is a broken piece of ancient pottery found at an archaeological site. Oftentimes, when we are broken, we know that only God can mend us, as he said, "Look unto me, and be ye saved, all the ends of the earth: for I am God, and there is none else" (Isaiah 45:22 KJV), "for great is our God above all gods" (2 Chronicles 2:5 KJV).

God is transcendent or almighty and extraordinarily above all things. Peace and Pruss (2012) explained that speaking of God as *omnipotent* means that he can do anything. When God is spoken of as being *omniscient*, it means that he knows everything. God's power is supreme and above everything, all-encompassing, and his power is unlimited!

God maintains a relationship with and through his people. This relationship is personal, interactive, and very real. It is an ongoing spiritual relationship that meets the needs of his people through Jesus Christ. This relationship is maintained through the people of God trusting and having faith in him, steadfast prayer, living by the Word of God through the Holy Spirit, and worshipping and praising him for all that he has done and all that he is going to do in their lives!

> Who hath saved us and *called* us with an *holy calling*, not according to our works, but according to *his own purpose* and *grace*, which was given us in Christ Jesus before the world began. (2 Timothy 1:9 KJV)

This is a general calling to salvation, to know God, and serve others (Thompson and Miller-Perrin 2003). He is "the Lord Almighty" (2 Corinthians 6:18 KJV).

God also calls us to *him* and to a specific purpose or mission for our life. This purpose in life includes our vocation, or our specific calling from God that goes far beyond our occupation or career. Vocation often includes serving others through what you do in your occupation or career. For example, if you feel that God led you into the field of teaching, nursing, or starting your own business to serve others, these and other occupations can be your vocation or calling. However, vocation generally means our *specific calling* and work in ministry, as well as our overall work in community, where the Holy Spirit leads us in serving others during our comprehensive day-to-day activities (Smith 2009; Thompson 2010; Thompson and Miller 2003).

In chapter 4, we will further explore walking in a *specific calling*, especially a prophetic calling and walking in your calling as a single/unmarried or never-married adult. Thompson and Miller-Perrin (2003) defined a specific calling as God's calling for you personally to walk in the assignment that you are given, whatever it is. God's purpose involves us serving others through our God-given gifts. Walking in your calling—whether single or married—requires dedication, a steadfast commitment to prayer, determination, perseverance, faith, patience, and trust in the Word of God!

> Faithful is he that calleth you, who also will do it. (1 Thessalonians 5:24 NIV)

> Being confident of this very thing, that he which hath begun a good work in you will perform it until the day of Jesus Christ. (Philippians 1:6 KJV)

ART, POTTERY, AND THE CLAY-HUMAN CONNECTION

A work of pottery art being molded and shaped
in the hands of an expert potter.

From a biblical perspective, God's purpose for his people centers
around their serving others through the use of their God-given gifts.

These pottery and ceramic pieces were created with a purpose in mind. What is your purpose in life?

Chapter 4

Exploring the Example of Jeremiah the Prophet

And God hath set some in the church, first apostles, secondarily prophets, thirdly teachers, after that miracles, then gifts of healings, helps, governments, diversities of tongues.
—1 Corinthians 12:28 KJV

There are five major prophets in the Old Testament: Isaiah, Jeremiah, Lamentations (because it is a book written by Jeremiah), Ezekiel, and Daniel. They are called the major prophets mainly because their books are substantially longer. The books of the major prophets are also said to have more global significance than the books of the twelve minor prophets: Hosea, Joel, Amos, Obadiah, Jonah, Micah, Nahum, Habakkuk, Zephaniah, Haggai, Zechariah, and Malachi (Stancil 2013). However, it must be kept in mind that all of the prophets are equally important since they are bringing a message that God has given to them (Carma 2017).

Jeremiah was born around 650 BCE or BC in a village called Anathoth. He grew up in a family of priests. His father, Hilkiah, was one of those priests (Jeremiah 1:1 KJV). The village of Anathoth was located slightly northeast of Jerusalem on the border between the southern kingdom of Judah and the northern kingdom of Israel. Jerusalem was the center of the northern kingdom of Israel (Hyatt 2020; Margalit 2018; Owens 1981; Youngblood 1990).

Prophets can also be referred to as seers. Through a special supernatural gift from God, by way of dreams, visions, picture images, words, inspirational thoughts, and scriptures, prophets *see* things that God is showing them that will help build up the body of Christ. From what they have seen, prophets/seers can give a prophetic message of encouragement and inspiration from God about how he is going to bless an individual or the collective church body, in a specific way, if they continue to trust and walk by faith in obedience to him. Prophecy benefits both believers and nonbelievers (Allen 2017; Bader 2017; Fairchild 2019, p. 1).

> Beforetime in Israel, when a man went to enquire of God, thus he spake, Come, and let us go to the seer: for he that is now called a Prophet was beforetime called a Seer. (1 Samuel 9:9 KJV)

For example, Gad was one of the personal seers (prophet) to King David in the Old Testament.

> Before David got up the next morning, the word of the Lord had come to Gad the prophet, David's seer: Go and tell David, This is what the Lord says: I am giving you three options. Choose one of them for me to carry out against you. (2 Samuel 24:11–12 NIV)

Called and equipped to be a prophet

Jeremiah is the author of the Bible's Old Testament book of Jeremiah, as well as the book of Lamentations that follows. Jeremiah prophesied (foretold) to Israel for forty years, during a six-hundred-year period before the birth of Jesus Christ, but his messages and prophecies are just as applicable today as they were then. God had called Jeremiah to be a prophet before he was born, as evidenced by the following scripture:

> Before I *formed* thee in the belly I knew thee; and before thou camest forth out of the womb I sanctified thee, and I *ordained* thee a prophet unto the nations. (Jeremiah 1:5 KJV)

The above powerful words from God to Jeremiah apply to all true prophets of God today.

Hogeterp (2018) emphasized that prophecy continues today to be a divine spiritual gift given by God for the work of the ministry. Apostle Paul, in his letter to the Ephesians, further clarified and explained that the primary purpose of prophecy was for the edifying (or enlightening, instructing, improving, and/or uplifting) of the church or the people of God:

> And he gave some, apostles; and some, *prophets*; and some, evangelists; and some, pastors and teachers; For the perfecting of the saints, for the work of the ministry, for the edifying of the body of Christ. (Ephesians 4:11–12 KJV)

As you can see, prophets are listed *second* after apostles as recorded in 1 Corinthians 12:28.

Clarke (2019) noted that the above two verses of scripture from the fourth chapter of the book of Ephesians are referring to those that are operating in their calling into the *office of a prophet* of God. The Spirit of God supernaturally gives the prophet the ability and power to speak the words of God in prophecy. Those called into the special office of a prophet of God would also, clearly and directly, apply to that scripture in Paul's first letter to the Corinthians:

> And God hath set some in the church, first apostles, secondarily prophets, thirdly teachers, after

> that miracles, then gifts of healings, helps, governments, diversities of tongues. (1 Corinthians 12:28 KJV)

> For as we have many members in one body, and all members have not the same office. (Romans 12:4 KJV)

God uses a prophet, or the prophetess (female prophet [Luke 2:36]), by speaking through them when he has a message for his people/a person or a message intended to be spread and applied to people anywhere in the world. Some referred to Jeremiah as the interpreter of God as he would, like other prophets, speak to the people on the behalf of God. A prophet of God was also referred to as a deliverer or one who brings God's words of warning and impending danger, as well as words of hope, release, healing, and deliverance. Overall, any true prophet of God is a spokesperson for God. The calling into the office of a prophet is a divine appointment (Fairchild 2019; Marchetti 2018; McConville 1991, p. 82; Youngblood 1990, p. 100).

The concept of prophecy, in general, was explained by Apostle Paul, who said:

> But the one who prophesies speaks to people for their strengthening, encouraging, and comfort. I would like every one of you to speak in tongues, but I would rather have you prophesy. The one who prophesies is greater than the one who speaks in tongues, unless someone *interprets* so that the church may be edified. (1 Corinthians 14:3, 5 NIV)

The relationship that prophets have with God is a close and spiritually intimate one of prayer and communion with the Holy Spirit. This leads prophets to spend much quiet time in fervent prayer, the Word of God, communication, praise, and fellowship with the Lord. This God-inspired ongoing prayer, study, and meditation on the scriptures and consistent fellowship and communion with the Holy Spirit become a consistent way of life for the prophet that results in scriptural revelations from the Word of God. These spiritual revelations may lead to a later prophetic word or message through the prophet from God (Jones 2018; LeClaire 2014).

> Knowing this first, that no prophecy of scripture is of any private interpretation. For the prophecy came not in old time by the will of man: but holy men of God spake as they were moved by the Holy Ghost. (2 Peter 1:20–21 KJV)

Spiritual "lockdown"

Prophets will not get with or go along with the corruption and/or traditions of men that they may see going on in the organized church and/or its leadership, including favoritism of some church members over others. We're not talking about honest and prayerful Spirit-led prioritizing of people in the ministry and work of the Lord. Favoritism is something different. Favoritism is *unfair* and *biased* preferential treatment given a person, or group of people, at the expense of someone else or others. For instance, have you ever felt that no matter how good and effective you were in a particular area, you were not going to be recognized or shown any kind of appreciation, no matter what you did, because it was you?

> Then Peter opened his mouth, and said, of a truth, I perceive that God is no respecter of persons: But in every nation he that feareth him, and worketh righteousness, is accepted with him. (Acts 10:34–35 KJV)

Many of us can remember certain of our school teachers or employers who showed partiality and favoritism toward one or more students/workers over other students or workers in the classroom or place of work in terms of grades, promotion, and/or how you were treated. This was, and still is, never viewed as a good classroom or workplace practice and tends to always cause resentment and animosity among others who may find themselves the victims of that kind of preferential and unfair treatment. These same kinds of negative feelings begin to fester in the church when members observe or feel that many decisions are made that are so obviously blatant and based on personal preference rather than on thoughtful spiritual consideration and prayer. However, whatever is going on around us, we must try not to focus on what man is doing or saying about us, but our focus should be on what God is doing and saying about us and that he knows all about our level of dedication and commitment to him.

God often sends the prophet into an intercessory/prophetic kind of prayer or a "stand in the gap" kind of prayer (Jacobs 1995).

> And I sought for a man among them, that should make up the hedge, and stand in the gap before me for the land, that I should not destroy it; but I found none. (Ezekiel 22:30 KJV)

This kind of committed, determined, God-inspired intercessory prayer is like an extended period of quiet time or a prayer *shelter-in-place, personal,* spiritual *lockdown* so that God can speak in an uninterrupted manner to the prophet. At the same time, the prophet can gain from this real and direct guidance by God in real time. For example, this is how the prophet Ezekiel described how God dealt with and spoke to him:

> Then the spirit entered into me, and set me upon my feet, and spake with me, and said unto me, Go, shut thyself within thine house. And I will

> make thy tongue cleave to the roof of thy mouth, that thou shalt be dumb, and shalt not be to them a reprover: for they are a rebellious house. But when I speak with thee, I will open thy mouth, and thou shalt say unto them, Thus saith the Lord God; He that heareth, let him hear; and he that forbeareth, let him forbear: for they are a rebellious house. (Ezekiel 3:24, 26–27 KJV)

God does not play favorites or show partiality toward certain persons or one group over another based on race, social status, gender, age, or marital status. Again, it cannot be overstated that whether Black, Brown, or White, young or old, or married or single, the Word of God assures us that we are validated, loved, and complete in him in *that* present status:

> But as God hath distributed to every man, as the Lord hath *called* every one, *so let him walk*. And so ordain I in all churches. (1 Corinthians 7:17 KJV)

> But now hath God set the members *every one of them* in the body, as it hath pleased him. But now are they many members, yet but one body. (1 Corinthians 12:18, 20)

Rainer (2014) reported that, for some church leaders, partiality and favoritism plays out in their systematic and willful tendency to surround themselves with a "favorite few" who may, or may not, be spiritually equipped for the position that they have been placed in or for the duties that they have been assigned to do. Conversely, Minnix (2005) respectfully urged that prioritizing speakers, projects, or who will do what in the church should be determined by sincere prayer and leading of the Holy Spirit. This can make a big difference in whether the occasion will be effective or not. No one should be excluded from any portion of a service for fear that they might get the credit for a move of God. It does not matter who God is moving through at any particular time because all the power, the credit, and the glory belongs to God!

No one can block or shut another person out of opportunities to be used by God and doors that God has already opened for them. The more he or she is ignored and pressed down by envy, jealousy, strife, and traditions of men, the more God will openly bless them and cause them to spring forth in what he has destined for them to do! The Old Testament story of how God protected his people when they were being oppressed by the Egyptians is an example of how God protects and causes his people to prosper today, even in times of trouble, distress, rejection, and any unfair treatment.

> But the more they were oppressed, the more they multiplied and spread, so the Egyptians came to dread the Israelites. (Exodus 1:12 NJV)

> I know thy works: behold, I have set before thee an open door, and no man can shut it: for thou hast a little strength, and hath kept my word, and hast not denied my name. (Revelation 3:8 KJV)

> Therefore, my beloved brethren, be ye stedfast, unmoveable, always abounding in the work of the Lord, forasmuch as ye know that your labour is not in vain in the Lord. (1 Corinthians 15:58)

The mission of the prophet is to—through steadfast and continued prayer, reliance on the Word of God, spiritual observation, ongoing praise, and the anointed empowerment, demonstration of, and obedience to the Holy Ghost—counteract that corruption and those traditions of men, including any hypocrisy and behaviors that are out of line with God's values. The hope is for *reformation* that God will return the hearts of his people back to him, not to a set of regulations, traditions, church leader, or any particular organized church (Bradley 2018; Butterfield 2018; Fairchild 2019; LeClaire 2014; Margalit 2018, p. 627; Woods 2014).

> But thou, *O man of God,* flee these things; and follow after righteousness, goodness, faith, love, patience, meekness. Fight the good fight of faith, lay hold on eternal life, whereunto thou art also called, and hast professed a good profession before many witnesses. (1 Timothy 6:11–12)

> For we wrestle not against flesh and blood, but against principalities, against powers, against the rulers of the darkness of this world, against spiritual wickedness in high places. (Ephesians 6:12 KJV)

LeClaire (2014) stressed that the prophet has a *reformation* mindset, or a mindset that seeks to bring about hope and change for the better for the people of God, by turning their hearts back to the Lord. God, through the Holy Spirit, gives the prophet revelations and a message in many different ways, including through prayer, scriptures, visions, and dreams. Prophets may be misunderstood as God will show them some things he has not shown others.

> Call unto me, and I will answer thee, and shew thee great and mighty things, which thou knoweth not. (Jeremiah 33:3 KJV)

> The prophet that hath a dream, let him tell a dream; and he that hath my word, let him speak my word faithfully. (Jeremiah 23:28 KJV)

> And when this cometh to pass, (lo, it will come,) then shall they know that a prophet hath been among them. (Ezekiel 33:33 KJV)

The prophet will speak what he sees and/or hears but will have to prayerfully and by faith take the chance of possible backlash, resentment, or being accused of being disagreeable against a certain leader, person, concept, or program. Nevertheless, prayerful prophets will let the Holy Spirit lead and guide them on how and when to speak what God has given them to speak.

> I will hear what God the Lord will speak: for he will speak peace unto his people, and to his saints but let them not turn again to folly. (Psalm 85:8 KJV)

Prophets usually have a quiet demeanor and are usually not seen hanging out with any particular group or clique unless God puts him or her with someone. Beware of labeling the prophet as antisocial or trying to make them fit into an organized box-like church prototype. God tells the prophet when to talk, when to be quiet, what to do, what not to do, when to come, when to go, where to go, and where not to go (See Jeremiah 16:1–5, 8, 10–12).

Whether intentional or unintentional, the prophet (or any church member) is caused hurt and harm when attempts are consistently made to coerce, embarrass, and/or pressure them into situations (including marriage) that God has not, or is not, leading them in to.

> It is an honour for a man to cease from strife: but every fool will be meddling. (Proverbs 20:3 KJV)

> But let none of you suffer as a murderer, or as a thief, or as an evildoer, or as a busybody, in other men's matters. (1 Peter 4:15 KJV)

Some people misunderstand and take out of context the scripture, "It is not good that the man be alone" (Genesis 2:18 KJV). When you *disconnect* one particular scripture from the scriptures around it or from the context of the thought in which the scripture was given, you miss the point of what the author was trying to convey. Thus, the reader who doesn't prayerfully consider the context in which Genesis 2:18 was given—or even one who doesn't know what other books in the Bible say about the subject—will automatically assume that this *one* scripture means that it is not good for *every* man not to have a wife. You don't have to be single to have feelings of loneliness or feelings of being alone. One can feel like they are alone or have feelings of loneliness even *with* a wife or *with* a husband (Collins 1976; Jepson 1970).

Many of us remember back in first-grade reading when we came across a word that we didn't know the meaning of, the teacher urged us to look at the familiar words, phrases, or pictures (*context* clues) around that unfamiliar word to try to figure out the meaning of the word (Nordquist 2020). It's the same with the Bible. You have to know what was going on in the scriptures before and after a particular scripture to avoid misinterpreting that scripture.

Genesis 2:18 is saying that it is not good for a person *not* to be known or not to have *any* kind of close personal ties, fellowship, and/or loving relationships with others, like extended family members, friends, school connections, classmates, coworkers, church friends where one is accepted as they are (Collins 1976). Most people then are not alone even if they live alone. We generally have people around us who love us, care about us, and are willing to help us in time of need. If Genesis 2:18 was saying that only marriage could fulfill the above-stated relationship needs for love, close personal ties, fellowship with, and help from others, the single or unmarried person in 1 Corinthians 7:32–34 would never have been reminded about how they can better focus, concentrate on, and wholeheartedly serve the Lord in their state of singleness (1 Corinthians 7:38) since they don't have the distractions that come along with being married.

Neither marriage nor singleness is a requirement from God for the believer (Minnicks 2020). *Both* marriage and singleness are good paths when either of the two paths is the one that a person feels is the calling of God for them that they are walking in at that time (Smith 2012).

> Who are *kept* by the power of God through faith unto salvation ready to be revealed in the last time. (1 Peter 1:5 KJV)

Thus, it is important for a believer to be prayerful, confident, and *led of the Lord* in whichever path or calling that they are walking, even when you're being talked about or in times of trouble.

> And we know that all things work together for good to them that love God, to them who are the *called* according to *his purpose*. (Romans 8:28 KJV)

It is important to have the *full understanding* of scripture in the *historical context* in which it was written (Kurz 2017). This full understanding of the context of any given scripture is needed before we start trying to direct that particular scripture unto a singled-out individual or group of people. Our *words matter,* especially when we don't have a full, contextual understanding of what we are talking about. And those words can hinder and hurt other people!

> Death and life are in the power of the tongue: and they that love it shall eat the fruit thereof. (Proverbs 18:21 KJV)

A word to the wise: Our prayer should be like David's prayer in the book of Psalms when he prayed, "Set a watch, O Lord, before my mouth; keep the door of my lips" (Psalm 141:3 KJV). In the New Testament book of James, this concept of how dangerous the tongue can be is further explored, addressed, and warned about where it says, "If any man among you seem to be religious, and bridleth not his tongue, but deceiveth his own heart, this man's religion is vain" (James 1:26 KJV). We must use wisdom and think before we speak.

Regarding wisdom, in the book of Proverbs, it goes on to stress that "wisdom is the principal thing; therefore get wisdom: and with all thy getting *get understanding*" (Proverbs 4:7 KJV). Romig (2019, p.1) described a biblical definition of wisdom as "skill for living." This skill for living takes place not by our way but by God's way by leaning on his Word. Wisdom is not only making the right choices, but it is also having a God-inspired character to make the right choices.

> Trust in the Lord with all thine heart; and *lean not unto thine own understanding*. In all thy ways acknowledge him, and *he* shall direct thy paths. (Proverbs 3:5–6 KJV)

The woman or man of God is very much aware of and in-tune with God's will for their life. They know how God is leading them regarding marriage/singleness or any other of life's personal decisions without having to deal with constant probing, implied innuendos (insinuations) about their sexuality, meddling, making them feel "less than," and making unkind public remarks and then laughing about it and trying to get others to laugh along with them. They're taking time out to try to be a comedian at the expense of someone else's feelings.

However, God provides protection against the unwarranted criticism and backlash from the tongues of others.

> You will be protected from the lash of the tongue, and need not fear when destruction comes. (Job 5:21 NIV)

In other words, when you are sincerely living in full commitment to God in your calling, and others take it upon themselves to use slanderous, vicious, and misguided words to talk about and describe you, God will protect you and deal with them. He will also lead you in how to deal with the situation, including what to say and what not to say. God's word promises that "no weapon that is formed against thee shall prosper; and every tongue that shall rise up against thee in judgment thou shalt condemn. This is the heritage of the servants of the Lord, and their righteousness is of me, saith the Lord" (Isaiah 54:17 KJV). Any kind of life-changing personal decision(s) for singles is best left to them and God, unless they seek out advice or volunteer to participate in any relevant and appropriate class or event that has been planned/scheduled for never-married singles or other categories of singles.

Jacobs (1995) likened putting someone through these kinds of trials and unpleasant experiences as a form of abuse or, as he referred to it, *spiritual abuse.* The main point is that if they (especially the singles/never marrieds) are joyfully claiming to have the victory, no one should be implying or treating them like they don't have the victory or that they're not as happy as somebody else thinks they should or could be. Maybe they would be happier if they didn't have to put up with being probed all the time and if they were accepted as they are.

These are troublesome, demeaning, and harmful circumstances to have to go through, especially in the church. But any man or woman of God will need to remember to pat themselves on the back, stay strong by praying through these circumstances, and continue to believe God's report about them, where happiness and being blessed are part of the package.

> Blessed is every one that feareth the Lord; that walketh in his ways. For thou shalt eat the labour of thine hands: happy shalt thou be, and it shall be well with thee. (Psalm 128:1–2 KJV)

In other words, the man or woman of God is just going to have to encourage themselves (Savelle 1998).

> But David encouraged himself in the Lord his God. (1 Samuel 30:6)

One special and spiritually enlightening quote about intimacy by a Christian evangelist, who was also an author, says, "A man who is intimate with God is not intimidated by man" (Leonard Ravenhill). Speaking lovingly, intimately, and affectionately about God in the book of Psalms, David, unapologetically and with conviction, proclaimed, "Whom have I in heaven but thee? And there is none upon earth that I desire beside thee" (Psalm 73:23, 25 KJV). Praise God! Now that's love!

Hold your head up and go on about your business, *trusting* and *believing* that God is able to protect and bless you as you keep walking in your calling. A man in the book of John asked Jesus to come to his house to heal his dying son. When Jesus told him that his son was healed right where they were standing, "the man *believed the word that Jesus had spoken unto him,* and he went his way" (John 4:50 KJV). The man started on his way back home without having to have Jesus physically come with him to his house. Before he got home, others met him who were eager to tell him that his son was healed. His son was healed at the same hour that Jesus had spoken it from afar off (John 4:51–53). Praise the Lord! Hallelujah!. To God be the glory!

Trust God in what *he* has already spoken about you! Daniel, when he had been cast into the lions' den, experienced how God can protect you from and shut certain mouths.

> Then said Daniel unto the king, O king, live for ever. My God hath sent his angel, and hath *shut the lions' mouths,* that they have not hurt me. (Daniel 7:21–22 KJV)

During our own troublesome situations, there is no need to worry or be afraid. God is able!

> And being fully persuaded [Abraham] that what he [God] had promised, he was able also to perform. (Romans 4:21 KJV)

What about when you go to bed at night? Does anyone need to be concerned about or have worries about how you are going to sleep? I don't think so, because the Word of God says, "When thou liest down, thou shalt not be afraid: yea, thou shall lie down, and *thy sleep shall be sweet"* (Proverbs 3:24 KJV). Don't worry about trying to please man. Just keep letting your light shine.

> When a man's ways *please the Lord*, he maketh even his enemies to be at peace with him. (Proverbs 16:7 KJV)

Some of you know this song, which is validated by scripture: "The Lord Will Make a Way Somehow."

> Behold, I will do a new thing; now it shall spring forth; shall ye not know it? *I will even make a way in the wilderness,* and rivers in the desert. (Isaiah 43:19 KJV)

High (2019) emphasized that we must come to grips with the fact that, for various reasons, some people don't get married. Simundson (2002) reported that, in the case of Jeremiah, God instructed and told him that he should not get married (see Jeremiah 16:1–2). "After all, in our culture we tend to make marriage the destination and singleness just part of the journey" (High, p.1). High went on to point out that the main emphasis of our calling and work for God and the legacy that we leave will not be on whether we were single or married. The core of our legacy will be on our heart for

God and our faithfulness and commitment that we exhibited to the calling and work that God has assigned us to carry out. Youngblood (1990) postulated that no one can be happier than an individual who has faithfully, willingly, and obediently answered their calling from the Lord with "here am I; send me" (Isaiah 6:8). Your true and special calling is by God's *grace,* so fully *embrace* it because there is no *disgrace* in it!

In times of any kind of trouble or unkind and outright mean words and actions from others, the Word of God is more than enough to encourage, strengthen, defend, protect, and *speak for you*! Remember the old saying, "It's in God's hands." Every situation that you have ever gone through, are going through, or will go through is like a piece of clay in God's hands! God is the protector, defender, the fence, hedge, or wall around us and the great potter who will mold, shape, rejuvenate, guide, and work everything out for us! God sees what's ahead of us long before we do and lightens our paths as we walk in them. What a mighty God we serve!

> When he giveth quietness, who then can make trouble? And when he hideth his face, who then can behold him? whether it be done against a nation, or against a man only. (Job 34:29 KJV)

As we walk in our calling, it is critically important that each of us take the time to study, contemplate on, and know what the Word of God says about us. Here are several scriptures for reference to build your faith and give you some interesting information that you may or may not have known was in the Bible (See 1 Corinthians 7:26–28, 32–33, 37–38). These scriptures show what it looks like to have and maintain God's *perspective* regarding the trials, tribulations, wrongdoing, and unjust actions that you may be facing at any given time (Caram 2010).

Remember, they tried to hurt Jesus, too—in the church!

> Then took they up stones to cast at him: but Jesus hid himself, and went out of the *temple*, going through the midst of them, and so passed by. (John 8:59 KJV)

The Lord will lead you when and how to get out when it's time to go!

> He suffered no man to do them wrong; yea, he reproved kings for their sakes: Saying, Touch not mine anointed, and do my prophets no harm (1 Chronicles 16:21–22; Psalm 105:14–15 KJV)

> The Lord shall fight for you, and ye shall hold your peace. (Exodus 14:14 KJV)

Remember to keep meditating on, having confidence in, and speaking what God is saying about you! Jesus said this about those who resist you in your walk with him.

> For I will give you words and wisdom that none of your adversaries will be able to resist or contradict. (Luke 21:15 NIV)

Also, believe that God is talking about you in his Word when he said, "I, even I, have spoken; yea; *I have called him*: I have brought him, and he shall make his way prosperous" (Isaiah 48:15 KJV).

Rejection of the prophet

> And the Lord hath sent unto you all his servants the prophets, rising early and sending them, but

> ye have not hearkened, nor inclined your ear to hear. (Jeremiah 25:4 KJV)

Prophets of God are often misunderstood, set aside, not accepted into certain ministerial circles, mocked, and fought against by some church leaders and/or some of the people. Prophets are often resented for not going along with traditions of men or for disagreeing with teachings that do not coincide with the Word of God. That man or woman of God should not get discouraged because "there is therefore now no condemnation to them which are in Christ Jesus, who *walk* not after the flesh, but after the Spirit" (Romans 8:1 KJV).

Those who do the mocking and rejecting are not only rejecting the prophet as a person, but they are rejecting any thoughts and God-inspired words or messages that the prophet may bring that they don't like. A true prophet is sent by God, so God is really the one being mocked and rejected. Jeremiah reminded the people of who sent him and why he was there: "For of a truth the Lord hath sent me unto you to speak all these words in your ears" (Jeremiah 26:15 KJV). Jesus understood this mockery and rejection well.

> But Jesus said unto them, A prophet is not without honour, save in his own country, and in his own house. (Matthew 13:57 KJV)

The prophet Isaiah so eloquently spoke and foretold about Jesus back in the Old Testament. Isaiah reminded us of how Jesus would suffer, be despised, wounded, and killed for our transgressions and how we would be healed, delivered, and set free by the beatings and stripes (wounds) that Jesus took in our place.

> He is despised and rejected of men: a man of sorrows, and acquainted with grief: and we hid as it were our faces from him; he was despised, and we esteemed him not. Surely he hath borne our griefs, and carried our sorrows: yet we did esteem

> him stricken, smitten of God and afflicted. But he was wounded for our transgressions, he was bruised for our iniquities: the chastisement of our peace was upon him; and with his stripes we are healed. (Isaiah 53:3–5 KJV)

Oftentimes, the attempt to hold the woman or man of God back is due to envy and/or jealousy of that woman or man of God. This results in them being overlooked, not recognized, and "put on the shelf" in the fear that the display of their anointing may cause them to outdo the person who is trying to stifle or thwart their influence. Smith (2014) defined jealousy as being threatened or intimidated by something you think you might lose. It is usually a person.

> Jealousy is cruel as the grave. (Song of Solomon 8:6 KJV)

Jealousy is usually about *someone.*
On the other hand, envy was defined as a person's reaction and/or behavior exhibited because of *something* they do not have or a higher level of something that they feel they don't have in comparison to someone else. LeClaire (2014) added that it is usually that envious person's own insecurity that keeps them from wanting to give recognition to the calling and gifts of another.

> Wrath is cruel, and anger is outrageous; but who is able to stand before envy? (Proverbs 27:4 KJV)

Irekamba (2015) further defined envy as where a person doesn't want someone to have something that God has given to him or her. I have learned over the years that *you don't have to stop shining just because someone is intimidated by your light!*

The following Bible scripture about charity (love) offers a very clear and direct eye-opening reminder for us: "Charity suffereth long, and is kind; charity envieth not; charity vaunteth not itself, is not puffed up" (1 Corinthians 13:4 KJV). In other words, the love of God leads us to be kind, appreciative, and thankful for how God is blessing and using us (and others) in who and what we are in him. In contrast to what envy can do to you, I thank God for peace and life.

> A heart at peace gives life to the body, but envy rots the bones. (Proverbs 14:30 NIV)

Jacobs (1995) noted the scripture that urges us to rejoice with those who are being blessed.

> Rejoice with them that do rejoice. (Romans 12:15 KJV)

Being envious of others is a result of a person comparing herself/himself to others, which leads that person to become spiteful and resentful of how God is blessing and using someone else. This is not good!

> Let us not be desirous of vain glory, provoking one another, envying one another. (Galatians 5:26 KJV)

> Wherefore laying aside all malice, and all guile, and hypocrisies, and envies, and all evil speakings. (1 Peter 2:1 KJV)

Just because you are rejected *does not* mean that you are not who *God* says you are and that *he* is not going to make a way for you to do what *he* has ordained!

Jeremiah's priority and desire was to walk in the ways of the Lord. He understood and obeyed God's calling for him. Although Jeremiah went through many painful and traumatic experiences, he continued to be prayerful and trusted in God's Word, knowing that

God was in control and would be with him in every situation in his life (Gordon 1903; Hoffeditz 2015).

> I know thy works: behold, I have set before thee an open door and no man can shut it: for thou hast a little strength, and hath kept my word, and hast not denied my name. (Revelation 3:8 KJV)

> Blessed is the man that trusteth in the Lord, and whose hope the Lord is. For he shall be as a tree planted by the waters, and that spreadeth out her roots by the river, and shall not see when heat cometh, but her leaf shall be green; and shall not be careful in the year of drought, neither shall cease from yielding fruit. (Jeremiah 17:7–8 KJV)

Comparable to Jeremiah 17:8, Psalm 1:3 says that whatsoever he does shall prosper.

In addition to the spiritual significance of a strong, budding, and flourishing tree, there is also an important spiritual significance that can be applied to the strength and usefulness of rock and the natural concept of the formation of clay. Clay is dug up out of soil after having been formed by the weathering of rock over long periods of time. Here are two scriptures that make an applicable analogy of the strength of rocks, in general, and the strength of God:

> The Lord is my *rock,* and my fortress, and my deliverer, my God, my strength, in whom I will trust; my buckler, and the horn of my salvation, and my high tower. (Psalm 18:2 KJV)

> And did all drink the same spiritual drink: for they drank of that spiritual *Rock* that followed them: and that *Rock* was Christ. (1 Corinthians 10:4 KJV)

A portion of the Christian song "My Hope Is Built on Nothing Less" by Edward Mote (1834), reads, "On Christ, the solid Rock, I stand; All other ground is sinking sand" (Hymnary 2007).

The prophet can sense the resistance, negative looks, and/or resentment coming from some church leaders, including some of the people. God comforted Jeremiah and assured him that he should not be afraid.

> Be not afraid of their faces: for *I am with thee* to deliver thee, saith the Lord. (Jeremiah 1:8 KJV)

That's why there's a familiar saying that goes, "if looks could kill, I'd be dead right now." Jeremiah spoke about his reaction to the looks, persecution, and painful experiences that he went through as a prophet and how the *Word of God* kept him:

> I sat not in the assembly of the mockers, nor rejoiced; I sat alone because of thine hand: for thou hath filled me with indignation. (Jeremiah 15:17 KJV)

> Then I said, I will not make mention of him, nor speak anymore in his name. But *his word* was in mine heart as a burning fire shut up in my bones, and I was weary with forbearing, and I could not stay. (Jeremiah 20:9 KJV)

> But *the Lord is with me* as a mighty terrible one: therefore my persecutors shall stumble, and they shall not prevail: they shall be greatly ashamed; for they shall not prosper: their everlasting confusion shall never be forgotten. (Jeremiah 20:11 KJV)

Validated, spiritually led, endorsed, and divinely inspired by God, the prophet goes forth anyway to proclaim a message and speak on behalf of God (Dein and Cook 2014; Woods 2014).

> But thou, O Lord, art a shield for me; my glory, and the lifter up of mine head. (Psalm 3:3 KJV)

Even through all kinds of adversity, backlash, jealousy, danger, hurt, resentment, and rejection, "a man's gift maketh room for him and bringeth him before great men" (Proverbs 18:16 KJV).

God backs up the prophet

God had already instructed Jeremiah, from back in the first chapter of the book of Jeremiah 1:8, not to be afraid, dismayed, or discouraged by the faces of the people (or by their looks) and their rejection. God reminded Jeremiah again later, saying, "And they shall fight against thee; but they shall not prevail against thee; for I am with thee, saith the Lord, to deliver thee" (Jeremiah 1:19 KJV). So Jeremiah went on to persevere, speak, and relay God's message to the people in Jeremiah 18:11, and they responded in verse 12.

> Thus saith the Lord; Behold I frame evil against you: return ye now every one from his evil way, and make your ways and your doings good. (Jeremiah 18:11 KJV)

> And they said, There is no hope: but we will walk after our own devices and we will every one do the imagination of his evil heart. (Jeremiah 18:12 KJV)

What may seem harsh to some, Jesus spoke a firm and direct response many years later to those who insisted on going on with their stubborn and wicked ways.

> Then he [Jesus] said unto them, *O fools*, and slow of heart to believe all that the prophets have spoken. (Luke 24:25)

One of Jeremiah's messages

Jeremiah prophesied to the people about how Babylon's king, Nebuchadnezzar, was going to march into Jerusalem and destroy and conquer Israel, which Jeremiah the prophet spake unto all the people of Judah and to all the inhabitants of Jerusalem, saying, "'Yet ye have not hearkened unto me,' saith the Lord, 'that ye might provoke me to anger with the works of your hand to your own hurt.'"

> Therefore thus saith the Lord of hosts; Because ye have not heard my words, Behold, I will send and take all the families of the north, saith the Lord, and Nebuchadnezzar the king of Babylon, my servant, and will bring them against this land, and against all these nations round about, and will utterly destroy them, and make them an astonishment, and an hissing, and perpetual desolations. (Jeremiah 25:2, 7–9 KJV)

> Nevertheless in those days, saith the Lord, I will not make a full end with you. (Jeremiah 5:18 KJV)

> And all the *vessels* of the house of God, great and small, and the treasures of the house of the Lord, and the treasures of the king and of his princes;

all these he brought to Babylon. (2 Chronicles 36:18 KJV)

However, God did not leave them without hope. "For thus saith the Lord, That after seventy years be accomplished at Babylon, I will visit you, and perform my good word toward you, in causing you to return to this place" (Jeremiah 29:10 KJV), but Babylon would have a dominate influence over the economic, agricultural, religious, and political world into the future for an estimated 2,500 years (Kranz 2014; Martin 1999).

> Shall a trumpet be blown in the city, and the people not be afraid? Surely the Lord God… revealeth his secret unto his servants the prophets. The lion hath roared, who will not fear? the Lord God hath spoken, who can but prophesy? (Amos 3:6–8 KJV)

God validates his word through miracles, signs, and wonders!

Through it all, the *theme* and feature story of the good news is that, just as the potter *restored*—reformed and reshaped the marred clay down at the potter's house (Jeremiah 18:4)—God can restore His people back to a godly and productive *relationship* with him. Please note that even when your things, artwork, treasured possessions, and other valuable personal items are taken during your fall or *setback*, God makes sure that everything that was taken from you will be restored in your *comeback*.

> And also let the golden and silver *vessels* of the house of God, which Nebuchadnezzar took forth out of the temple which is at Jerusalem, and brought unto Babylon, be *restored,* and brought again unto the temple which is at Jerusalem,

> everyone to his place, and place them in the house of God. (Ezra 6:5 KJV)

What about the years that were wasted and lost with your involvement with so many unproductive things you thought you had to have?

> And I will *restore* to you the years that the locust hath eaten, the cankerworm, and the caterpillar, and the palmerworm, my great army which I sent among you. (Joel 2:25 KJV)

Praise God! Because of all of this, I have made up my mind that I'm gonna sing my love song to him, "speaking to yourselves in psalms and hymns and spiritual songs, singing and making melody in your heart to the Lord" (Ephesians 5:19 KJV).

The title of this book, *Art, Pottery, and the Clay-Human Connection: Understanding the Prophet Whom God Has Set in the Church!* was chosen because the Bible uses clay and the art of pottery to show the strong connection between clay, being shaped under the control of the hands of a potter, and man being formed and shaped under the control of and in the hands of God. Jeremiah, and his calling to be a prophet, was used as a perfect example of this special clay-human connection scenario, including his steadfast commitment to walk in his calling. Our clay-human experiences, testimonies, and our stories can have a profound and positive impact on others as our experiences, testimonies, and stories serve as an encouragement and life-saving testament to people from all walks of life. We often never know about the many people we have helped just by saying something about what God has done for us.

> Let the redeemed of the Lord say so, whom he hath redeemed from the hand of the enemy. (Psalm 107:2 KIV)

DR. ALVIN HAYWOOD, ED.D.

"But now, O Lord, thou art our father: we are the clay, and thou our potter; and we all are the work of thy hand" (Isaiah 64:8 KJV).

Believe in your calling

Looking through the lens of a Christian believer's viewpoint, knowing your purpose in life gives you insight into your calling and the confidence to walk in it.

I believe in my calling, with all of its assignments,
including the writing of this book.
Dr. Alvin Haywood

Chapter 5

A New Kind of 3 Rs: Release, Restoration, Revival

I waited patiently for the Lord; and he inclined unto me, and heard my cry. He brought me up also out of an horrible pit, out of the miry clay, and set my feet upon a rock, and established my goings.
—Psalm 40:1–2 KJV

Traditional methods of teaching

Traditional methods of teaching reading, writing, and math were through placing a main focus on phonics, diagramming sentences, copying writing exercises, memorizing a large number of math and other facts, and sitting and listening to the teacher for the majority of class time. These teaching strategies and concentration on rote learning, in those three core subject areas, was called the "three Rs" or reading, writing, and arithmetic. It was well-known that they were so named because each subject started with an R speech sound (Alisma and McGuire 2015). The focus of assessment, testing, and student evaluation was on one-time summative assessments and tests that took place at the end of study units, grading periods, or at the end of the school year assessments which may (or may not) have been aligned with what had actually been taught in the classroom during that academic school year. Students were then ranked and compared with one another by test scores. Assessment was considered separate from instruction (Cauley 2010; Clark 2008).

Having taught at the elementary and middle school levels, during those "three Rs" traditional ways of teaching and beyond, I can attest to a few more traditional approaches that were prevalent during those times. The subject-matter textbook was the main medium of instruction. These textbooks were accompanied by workbooks where children were guided through and required to complete pages and pages of drill-type matching and fill-in-the-blank exercises. In most cases, especially from third or fourth grade on, students sat in rows of five or six students across the classroom. Unless you raised your hand to speak, being quiet and staying in your seat was encouraged, as opposed to the twenty-first-century classroom where seating is arranged that allows for active student participation and meaningful open dialogue among students and with the teacher. Textbooks are still used but as one of many vehicles for delivering instruction. Those other more contemporary, effective, and flexible methods of instruction and learning are highlighted in the following two sections on clay art studio learning and twenty-first-century learning.

Clay art studio learning

The art studio space, in the context of learning by doing, provides a platform for integrating academics with relevant project-based creative art activities. These creative art activities include clay work (Corazzo 2019). For example, clay work and ceramics can spark ideas for enhancing and developing on-task engagement, positive student interaction, communication, collaboration, and effective writing skills (Sessions 1997).

Those with good writing skills are clear in their writing. Clarity in writing results in the reader being able to understand the message that the writer is attempting to convey. One aspect of being clear in your writing includes carefully proofreading and editing your work to make sure that your readers are not discouraged or turned off from reading your work because of uncorrected spelling, punctuation, and/or grammar errors. Overall, effective and skillful writers *plan* what they want to say ahead of time. They *translate* their plan of organized ideas into structured written text, and they *check* and *revise* what they have written as needed.

Having good writing skills is a springboard to good writing. Another aspect of good and purposeful writing is where the writer or author is willing to share one or more of their heartfelt life experiences. This can be in the form of a story that the writer feels are important to communicate to others (Buyer 2013; Ferrari, Bouffard, Rainville 1998; Solheim 2018).

It is exciting to know that God can give you a writing assignment. This is encouraging to me, as I know that *writing this book* was an assignment that was given to me from the Lord, and I was eager to get started on it and bring it to completion. Bader (2017) pointed out and affirmed that, in addition to God's gift of prophecy, many prophets have also been given the gift of writing for the purpose of seeing and transcribing what God is saying over time.

> The word that came to Jeremiah from the Lord, saying, Thus speaketh the Lord God of Israel, saying, *Write thee all the words that I have spoken unto thee in a book.*(Jeremiah 30:1–2 KJV)

Personally, when I am writing, I am "speaking" to the page and translating my thoughts onto that page on which I am writing. Like David in the book of Psalms, I feel motivated, validated, inspired, and convinced that "my tongue is the pen of a ready writer" (Psalm 45:1 KJV).

The learning environment in a clay art studio can provide some valuable insight into some instructional approaches and practices that can have a fundamental impact on increasing student engagement, enhancing interdisciplinary learning, creating a sense of belonging, making time for opportunities to share, and the realization of positive achievement outcomes across the core subject areas of reading, writing, mathematics, science, and history. Art studio learning strategies, such as a balance between student-free exploration and teacher-guided instruction, enhance students' overall learning experiences. Active involvement of students in projects of personal interest, hands-on learning, a focus on enjoyment (not ability), letting students know that taking risks and making mistakes are part of the learning process, and allowing students to act on their creative ideas also enhances overall learning and has a positive impact on increasing students' social and academic achievement (Albertson and Davidson 2009). Thinking about the use of technology through the lens of high-speed computers in many classrooms today, it is interesting to note its connection to the traditional potter's wheel, which is considered to be the first machine invented back in ancient times (Staubach 2005).

Twenty-first century learning

In today's twenty-first-century classrooms, instructional strategies for teaching the three Rs focus more on actively involving children in their learning and assessment in an attempt to balance teacher-direct instruction with guided exploratory student learning. Relevant math, writing, and reading strategies (like phonics) are used in the context of real-life stories and in real science and historical cultural events. Technology is used as a tool for motivating students and increasing their overall higher-level thinking skills and meaningful learning. Computer-aided instruction (CAI) can be used to create instructional design plans that are structured in ways to address a variety of learning styles and meet the needs of a variety of differentiated and diverse learning needs of students in the classroom.

In our increasingly technological society, students are given more choice in choosing topics that are interesting to them across core subjects. Students are also encouraged to participate in small group inquiry-based, hands-on learning projects with their peers. Project-based and hands-on learning experiences, as a part of an overall teaching strategy design program, sharpen students' tactile-kinesthetic motor sensations and evokes deep critical thinking in the context of positive release of their creative imagination, communication, and collaborative skills; emotional expression; and their productivity in and out of the classroom.

As opposed to a concentration on one-time summative assessments and tests, *formative* assessments are used that take place during instruction. Students are observed, monitored, and given ongoing feedback on their mastery of skills that are being taught at that time. With formative assessment, there is a de-emphasis on comparing students with one another with more emphasis and a focus on mastery of targeted skills, reaching set learning goals, and learning from one's mistakes. Thus, assessment guides instruction as assessment is integrated with instruction. Formative assessment and instructional practice become a seamless and interactive process that support student learning and overall authentic academic performance and achievement. This emphasis on actively involving students in relevant core subject-learning activities and involving them in monitoring and evaluating their own mastery of learning goals through formative assessment is important for increasing student motivation and classroom engagement. When learning activities involve some choice, feelings of pride, personal interest, and a sense of confidence and empowerment, then motivation is increased. Increased motivation results in increased productivity, creative exploration, genuine learning, and increased student learning and achievement (Alvermann, Gillis, and Phelps 2013; Cauley 2010; Clark 2008; Clark 2015; Elbrecht and Antcliff 2014; Hocine, Zhang, Song, and Ye 2014; Lusebrink 2004; Ovidiu-Iliuta 2013; Pang 2009; Tranquillo 2008). Getting students prepared for the twenty-first-century workplace requires some careful reimagination and rethinking of what students really need. Students not only need to be able to navigate a subject-matter textbook, learn basic and relevant facts, and take tests, but they also need opportunities to build their communication, collaborative, negotiation, and higher-level thinking skills (Pang 2009).

As for children and art museums, a school field trip to an art museum should have those same twenty-first-century goals of cultural inclusion, active involvement, opportunities for some choice of activities, building communication skills, and increased motivation. We all bring our own knowledge and lived cultural experiences to the interpretation of any given piece of artwork. Some art museums are allowing children to spontaneously respond to the art exhibits according to their own experiences and interests. This flexible strategy approach has an impact on the children's interpretations of certain works of art, including pottery and ceramics.

Ancient pottery finds are the most common historical articles of cultural value for archaeologists. Studying and finding out what the piece of pottery was specifically used for is extremely important. Pottery vessels were used for many purposes across a wide range of activities. Children can and should be a part of that conversation as to how they think pottery vessels were used back in ancient times. The insight and input of children are important.

One flexible art museum field trip strategy that has had positive outcomes is having children serve as tour guides for small groups of their classmates and/or groups of parents. This strategy, like in a regular innovative and child-centered classroom setting, promotes active involvement and exploration, increased motivation, inquiry learning, and the building of communication skills around real pieces of artwork and art history. The children are prepared ahead of time for their tour guide experience by having them spend some informal time with selected artists whose work is on display at the museum. They hear the artist's feelings about how they came up with their creative artwork and how they worked on it and brought it to completion. The children learn about and connect various works of art through a balanced student-inquiry approach, as opposed to only listening to facts and art lectures. In this way, the children can ask questions of designated artists while constructing and adding some of their own interpretations and meaning about the artwork. Without having to feel like they have to be at a prescribed ability level, young children, during their interactive sessions with selected artists and during their stint as a tour guide, can be "simply asked to talk about or explain what they thought and felt about the art they viewed" (Ellison 1984; Weier 2004, p. 107).

Clay has long been a critical component for sustaining human life around the world (Konta 1995). Back in the time of ancient civilizations, the major teaching strategy for learning crafts and making pottery was for the learner to learn by doing. For example, the Pueblo people of the Ancestral Pueblo in the American Southwest learned how to recognize good clay materials, how to extract the clay from the earth, where to find water, and how to transport the bulk clay materials to where they would be shaped and formed into desired pottery and ceramic objects.

Regarding Pueblo children, learning took place in the context of play and helping the adults with pottery projects. The children took small pieces of clay and made toys out of it. There was an interconnectedness among the concepts of play, learning, and work. (Crown 2014). Some writers have called and described the adult potters as folk or traditional potters because they learned their pottery-crafting skills in a practical home, hands-on environment (Burrison 2017). All students should have an education that is connected to real life.

Jeremiah's *trip* down to the potter's house (Jeremiah 18:1–6) was like a personalized *field trip*. God instructed Jeremiah by providing him with a natural hands-on lesson. This lesson, conducted by the potter in real time, had a true and profound spiritual significance! This coincides with the importance of real-life, relevant, and meaningful learning experiences.

> The steps of a good man are ordered by the Lord;
> and he delighteth in his way. (Psalm 37:23 KJV)

At the beginning of this chapter 5, we looked back at and reviewed the traditional methods that involved the teaching of the three Rs: reading, writing, and arithmetic. We remember and noted that those subjects were called the three Rs because they started with the R sound. In the context of Jeremiah's prophetic calling to Israel, this chapter 5 will now look at another kind of three Rs from a biblical/Christian perspective: *release*, *restoration*, and *revival*. These three

Rs are important biblical concepts and principles throughout the Bible and in this book.

Release

Release, or to be released, is one of the critical components among the other two biblical three Rs—restoration and revival. Release is where one experiences release from confining circumstances, whether that confinement was physical in real time or whether the confinement was in the mind. Real release gives you the freedom to move, act, and live freely—in your body, mind, and spirit—without fear or condemnation.

> There is therefore now no condemnation to them which are in Christ Jesus, who walk not after the flesh, but after the Spirit. (Romans 8:1 KJV)

> For in him we live, and move, and have our being. (Acts 17:28 KJV)

Release also includes letting go of things, certain circumstances of life, and even some people that we need to *release ourselves from* or walk away from. We're talking about negative things, some people, and situations that are holding us back from moving forward and making progress. Release of some things, people, and situations are just as important as adding on positive things, ideas, and positive people in our lives who may help us grow. Thus, while we may need to lose or let go of some things, there is always room for keeping and/or adding on so many other positive situations and circumstances in our lives.

> A time to cast away stones, and a time to gather stones together; a time to embrace, and a time to refrain from embracing; a time to get, and a time

to lose; a time to keep, and a time to cast away. (Ecclesiastes 3:5–6 KJV)

One of the most miraculous and prime examples of release is when Jesus raised Lazarus from the dead.

> Then they took away the stone from the place where the dead was laid. And Jesus lifted up his eyes, and said, Father, I thank thee that thou hast heard me. And when he thus had spoken, he cried with a loud voice, Lazarus come forth. And he that was dead came forth, bound hand and foot with graveclothes: and his face was bound about with a napkin. Jesus saith unto them, Loose him, and let him go. (John 11:41, 43–44 KJV)

Lazarus was loosed, or released.

> If the Son therefore shall make you free, ye shall be free indeed. (John 8:36 KJV)

Once a person or a group of people have been released and set free from a particular confinement and/or oppressive circumstances, they can go on to be *restored* or brought back into a desired state of freedom. However, spiritually speaking, God's freedom and his presence can be experienced by a person even when they are in confinement before they are physically released.

> God is our refuge and strength, a very *present help in* trouble. (Psalm 46:1 KJV)

ART, POTTERY, AND THE CLAY-HUMAN CONNECTION

Restoration

Restoration, or to be restored, is one of the backbone concepts of a biblical perspective and desire of the Christian believer. No matter what you are facing, what the problem is, or what you are going through, God has promised that if we stay with him or turn back to him, he will always restore us back to what or where we should be in him. Jesus said, "Him that cometh to me I will in no wise cast out" (John 6:37 KJV). In the book of Psalms, David said, "He *restoreth* my soul: Yea, though I walk through the valley of the shadow of death, I will fear no evil: for thou art with me; thy rod and thy staff they comfort me" (Psalm 23:3–4 KJV).

In your trying and difficult situation and circumstances, keep saying and singing to yourself that God is going to turn it around!

> Thou hast turned for me my mourning into dancing: thou hast put off my sackcloth, and girded me with gladness. (Psalm 30:11 KJV)

Many of us have been urged to—through words, scriptures, and songs—hold on to God's unchanging hand.

> Hold on to what you have, so that no one will take your crown. (Revelation 3:11 NJV)

It is very important not to forget to remember that when pottery containers and dishes get broken, they are generally thrown away. Like pottery containers, people also become broken at times. Just because something or someone has been broken doesn't mean that it/they should be thrown away or considered as garbage. People should certainly never be looked upon as garbage! Many of us have many times been broken by one or more of life's circumstances and have scars or bruises that we may have been trying to hide. Always remember what Paul said the Lord told him when he was going through trials and persecutions that came along with his doing what God had called him to do: "And he said unto me, *My grace is sufficient for thee*: for my strength is made perfect in weakness" (2 Corinthians 12:9 KJV). In fact, when you may be feeling weak and/or broken, speak the words that the Word of God advises you to speak: "Let the weak say, I am strong" (Joel 3:10 KJV).

> I will go in the strength of the Lord God: I will make mention of thy righteousness, even of thine only. (Psalm 71:16 KJV)

Hurt and broken people can be anywhere, including in the church (Walton 2017). David identified with broken containers or vessels when he was going through some hard circumstances that he had brought upon himself—hard circumstances and troubles that seemed to be weighing him down. He said, "I am forgotten as though I were dead; I have become like broken pottery" (Psalm 31:12 NIV). David continued on in a later scripture, "Though you have made me see troubles, many and bitter, you will *restore* my life again; from the depths of the earth you will again bring me up" (Psalm 71:20 NIV). Continuing to speak of the goodness of God, David later went on to further proclaim: "He healeth the broken in heart, and bindeth up their wounds" (Psalm 147:3 KJV). If you ever feel hurt, broken, and beyond repair, God is the one who will pick you up, restore, renew, and put you back together again.

> For the Lord taketh pleasure in his people: he will beautify the meek with salvation. (Psalm 149:4 KJV)

Because of Jeremiah's steadfast faithfulness and commitment to his calling as a prophet, his willingness to speak what God had told him to speak, and his adamant refusal to go along with organizational church protocol, which was often not according to the word of God, Jeremiah continued to be rejected, ridiculed, beaten, and imprisoned. He was even cast down into a dungeon that was located in the prison. In spite of all of this, God was with Jeremiah, kept him alive, never left him, protected him, spoke to him, and used him for the glory of God *while* he was in prison. God is there even in our most difficult, troublesome, and trying times.

> Moreover the word of the Lord came unto Jeremiah the second time, while he was yet shut up in the court of the prison, saying, Behold, I will bring it health and cure, and I will cure them [revive], and reveal unto them the abundance of peace and truth. And I will cause the captivity of Judah and the captivity of Israel to return [release], and will build them [restore], as at the first. And I will cleanse them from all their iniquity, whereby they have sinned against me; and I will pardon all their iniquities, whereby they have sinned, and whereby they have transgressed against me. (Jeremiah 33:1, 6–8 KJV)

The time that Jeremiah was cast down into a dungeon in the prison, God provided for his release just in time!

> Then they took Jeremiah and cast him into the dungeon of Malchiah the son of Hammeelech, that was in the court of the prison. And in the dungeon there was no water, but mire: so Jeremiah sunk in the mire. Then the king commanded Ebedmelech the Ethiopian, saying, Take from hence thirty men with thee, and take up Jeremiah the prophet out of the dungeon, before he die. So they drew up Jeremiah with cords and took him up out of the dungeon: and Jeremiah remained in the court of the prison. (Jeremiah 38:6, 10, 13 KJV)

However, Jeremiah was later released from the prison and his prophetic ministry continued.

> The Lord will vindicate me; your love, Lord, endures forever—do not abandon *the works of your hands*.(Psalm 138:8 NIV)

This scripture, among so many others, gives me courage to know that God made me, and his Word will keep me in and through all circumstances. David the psalmist also firmly and confidently proclaimed, "When I cry unto thee, then shall mine enemies turn back: this I know; for God is for me" (Psalm 56:9 KJV). *Hallelujah!* Praise God!

Even when we feel that we are down in the "dungeon," psychologically, spiritually, or any other way, God always comes in and brings us release and restores us back to the place where we should be! God often gives us even more than we had before. After Job's devastating illness and other tragedies, the word of God says, "And the Lord turned the captivity of Job. Also, the Lord gave job twice as much as he had before. So the Lord blessed the latter end of Job more than his beginning" (Job 42:10, 12 KJV). God is able, and he always steps in just in time and does what needs to be done.

> I have made the earth, and created man upon it: I even *my hands* have stretched out the heavens, and all their host have I commanded. (Isaiah 45:12 KJV)

Revival

For the children of Israel, it was a spiritual awakening for them, knowing that if they would turn back to God, they would be able to live in a way that was a more safe and productive way, even after their rebellion against Jeremiah's earlier prophecy (Jeremiah 25:2, 7–9). According to the continued *theme* of this book, clay in the hands of the potter is like man in the hands of God. It was God's promise and merciful *hands* that would be the major factor in the reviving and *reshaping* of the lives of the people of God, just like it was the potter's hands that were instrumental in the reshaping of the piece of clay.

> And I will deliver thee out of the hand of the wicked, and I will redeem thee out of the hand of the terrible. (Jeremiah 15:21 KJV)

God is not only a master potter in the studio, but he can also be your doctor in the sickroom, your negotiator in the boardroom, and your lawyer and defender in a courtroom.

> Therefore thus saith the Lord; Behold, I will plead thy cause, and take vengeance for thee. (Jeremiah 51:36 KJV)

In the book of Psalms, David gave a touching response: "Wilt thou not revive us again: that thy people may rejoice in thee?" (Psalm 85:6 KJV). God can even restore and revive youthfulness in his people, making them strong and lively again.

> Who satisfieth thy mouth with good things; so that thy youth is renewed like the eagle's. (Psalm 103:5 KJV)

From a Christian New Testament perspective, revival is a Christian believer (or the church—collective body of Christ) returning to a full sincerity in serving God in prayer, praise, studying, and meditating on God's word and obeying God's word under the leadership, guidance, and help of the Holy Spirit. Revival is an improvement in areas of your life that causes you to become active or alive again! You and/or the church are revived or spiritually reinstated back to where you once were in serving God (Budiselic 2014; Grace House 2015).

Speaking of the Holy Spirit, Apostle Paul said, "Now the Lord is that Spirit: and where the Spirit of the Lord is, there is liberty" (2 Corinthians 3:17 KJV). Queiroz (2018) described liberty in the context of one being generally *free*, as opposed to being a servant to some arbitrarily appointed person/dictator, group of people, or a government. On the other hand, Apostle Paul was speaking in a biblical or spiritual context where liberty or spiritual freedom is found in Christ Jesus.

> Stand fast therefore in the *liberty* wherewith Christ hath made us *free,* and be not entangled again with the yoke of bondage. (Galatians 5:1 KJV)

In other words, if Christ has released, restored, revived, and made you free by his word, why should you allow yourself to be bound by any of your circumstances?

> The word of God is not bound. (2 Timothy 2:9 KJV)

Revival makes everything as good as new!

> O sing unto the Lord a new song; for he hath done marvelous things: his right hand, and his holy arm has gotten him the victory. (Psalm 98:1 KJV)

Keep on singing that new song as you stay in revival mode and walk in your purpose and calling. Trust is one of the key ingredients for moving forward in the Lord.

> Blessed are all they that put their trust in him. (Psalm 2:12 KJV)

Yes, just trust him by faith! God is a good God, and he knows who is and who is not putting their confidence and trust in him.

> The Lord is good, a strong hold in the day of trouble, and he knoweth them that trust in him. (Nahum 1:7 KJV)

Whatever our status is in life, we have everything we need in Christ Jesus to walk in our calling.

> His divine power has given us *everything* we need for a godly life through our knowledge of him who called us by his own glory and goodness. (2 Peter 1:3 NIV)

No child of God is lacking or missing anything. We are fully equipped and qualified in him! God will provide! I am always in remembrance of the following two scriptures:

> I had fainted, unless I had believed to see the goodness of the Lord in the land of the living. Wait on the Lord; be of good courage, and he shall strengthen thine heart: wait, I say, on the Lord. (Psalm 27:13–14 KJV)

Creating beautiful works of pottery art, sorting, categorizing, analyzing, and keeping inventory of completed objects are just a few of the duties of a professional potter.

ART, POTTERY, AND THE CLAY-HUMAN CONNECTION

The Japanese art practice, kintsukuroi, is about repairing and restoring broken pottery by putting the pieces back together with a dusted silver or gold material. People, like pottery, become broken, too, but that doesn't mean that either one needs to be "thrown away." Regarding people, God specializes in restoring and putting his people back together again.

Chapter 6

Conclusion

And he that sat upon the throne said, Behold, I make all things new. And he said unto me, *Write*: for these words are true and faithful.
—Revelation 21:5 KJV

Clay is a valuable mineral that has served a variety of human household and industrial purposes and needs down through the years from ancient and biblical times. Pottery was first used around 14,000 BC for storing food, indicating group affiliation, and expressing one's artistic talents by painting designs on pottery items. Clay tablets were formed for writing and keeping records. Clay also continues to be used for manufacturing various industrial products, for some home construction, and for creating beautiful pottery and ceramic works of art.

Working with clay and getting involved with pottery at some point in one's life has a number of benefits for both children and adults. Many of us can remember, as young children, the joys of having our own piece of clay or Play-Doh to create whatever we wanted and however we wanted to create it. You were in control of what you were making, and you could work at your own pace without any pressure to come up to some skill or ability level in competition with others unless it was a known and voluntary competitive contest activity. These fond, exploratory, free-flowing clay activity memories may have continued if you had opportunities to participate in community arts programs or take different-leveled pottery classes at school as you advanced through grade-level arts and craft courses that were offered.

Formal and/or informal experiences with clay and pottery, whether at home, at school, or through community-based programs, provide opportunities for developing communication, collaboration, and social skills, as well as opportunities for aiding and strengthening small and large muscle development. Regarding young children, increased communication skills and small and large muscle development prepares children for writing, reading, mathematics, and other academic skills needed for success in school. For all ages, participation in pottery and other arts programs, especially those sponsored by the community, also provides a venue for making new friends across age, education, career, ethnic, socioeconomic, status, and artistic ability levels.

Art, such as clay work and pottery, is an exploration of the human experience and sets the stage for this book's theme: *the clay-human connection*. The Bible uses clay, being shaped under the control of and in the hands of a potter, to provide clear, natural, and meaningful imagery of the spiritual significance of a believer who is under the control and in the hands of God to be formed, molded, and shaped by him. Taking time to understand and appreciate how art and pottery transcend across so many aspects of our lives is critical for connecting the natural and spiritual aspects of those artistic and creative experiences to our everyday living.

To show this spiritually significant clay-man connection, God sent Jeremiah the prophet down to the potter's house to observe a hands-on lesson of the potter working with a piece of clay on the potter's wheel (Jeremiah 18:1–6). Modern-day students are taken on field trips to observe real people engaging in work that they have read about in their school books. Jeremiah, in a sense, was sent by God on his own special and individual field trip. The moral of the pottery lesson for Jeremiah is revealed in Jeremiah 18:6. God gives Jeremiah a prophetic word/message for the church, or the people of God, by asking, "O house of Israel, cannot I do with you as this potter? Saith the Lord. Behold, as the clay is in the potter's hand, so are ye in mine hand, O house of Israel" (Jeremiah 18:6 KJV). This scripture is the biblical perspective of ancient art, pottery, the clay-human connection, and walking in a prophetic calling, which is the substance of the title of this book. The power and authority of the Word of God is the voice of truth, a map, and a guide that casts light on the path of the believer.

> Thy word is a lamp unto my feet, and a light unto my path. (Psalm 119:105 KJV)

Jesus said, "I am the way, the truth, and the life: no man cometh unto the Father but by me" (John 14:6 KJV).

Prophets are often passionate and resourceful writers! In many instances, God will tell the prophet to write down the message that he is giving them through inspirational thoughts, prayer, scripture, dreams, or through visions for future reference for an upcoming prophecy.

> And the Lord answered me, and said, *Write the vision,* and make it plain upon the tables, that he may *run* that readeth it. (Habakkuk 2:2 KJV)

Those who hear or read a prophetic message coming straight from the mouth of the Lord will *run* with excitement to tell others about it.

The prophet Isaiah was also instructed by God to write what God was saying and why: "Now go, *write* it before them in a table, and *note it in a book,* that it may be for the time to come for ever and ever" (Isaiah 30:8 KJV). Prophecy is for the present time and to the people to whom it is spoken, but sometimes the prophecy is for future times and may happen years later. As for me and my enthusiasm for the writing and speaking of my own God-given prophetic messages and sharing stories of my personal victories and triumphs over life-threatening trials and tribulations, I am inspired to let verses of scripture lead and guide me. I am encouraged by those people in the Bible with whom I can connect.

> My heart is stirred by a noble theme as I recite my verses for the king; my tongue is the pen of a skillful writer. (Psalm 45:1 NJV)

The focus of this book is on the example of Jeremiah and his commitment to his calling as a prophet and how he endured and overcame many ongoing incidents of rejection, mocking, resistance, persecution, and outright physical violence.

> For whatsoever is born of God overcometh the world: and this is the victory that overcometh the world, even our faith. (1 John 5:4 KJV)

This book also focuses on the trials and triumphs of the single or unmarried person. Jeremiah was single (Jeremiah 16:1–2) as he walked in his prophetic calling. However, this book's subject matter and overall content is also beneficial for the church at large and *anyone* who is diligently and faithfully walking and operating in *any* ministry or calling of God.

In addition to any prophet experiencing rejection simply because the prophet is speaking a prophecy or message from God that the people may not like, the single/unmarried or never married prophet of God (or any single adult believer) will often also have to endure being misunderstood and probed about their marital status. They are often rejected, pressured to consider marrying a person that someone else has picked out for them, have disparaging questions and intimidating remarks directed at them, and are often subjected to ongoing insinuations that they are alone, incomplete, and not as happy as their married counterparts.

Much of the time, those who engage in these demeaning and confrontational behaviors toward others don't even realize that it is often *their own* misunderstanding of scripture and *their own* attitude and behaviors toward that single person that are usually what is causing heartache, feelings of not being fully accepted, and any resulting unhappiness for that single adult congregant or church member. But David said, "Mine eyes are ever toward the Lord; for he shall pluck my feet out of the net" (Psalm 25:15 KJV). As we prayerfully and diligently study the Word of God for instruction, guidance, strength, and comfort, our sincere prayer should be that he will give us *spiritual clarification* and *understanding* of all scripture.

> Then opened he [Jesus] their understanding, that they might understand the scriptures. (Luke 24:25 KJV)

> If an enemy were insulting me, I could endure it; if a foe were rising against me, I could hide it. But it is you, a man like myself, my companion, my close friend, with whom I once enjoyed sweet fellowship at the house of God, as we walked about among the worshipers. (Psalm 55:12–14 NIV)

By divine inspiration, this book promotes the idea of confidently knowing and boldly speaking what God (not people) says about you, whether someone is operating out of misunderstanding of the scriptures or not. This confidence includes the resisting of the traditional and stereotypical verbal and behavioral attacks against your single, faithful, and committed walk with the Lord. *God accepts you just as you are in your present status*!

> I will accept you with your sweet savour. (Ezekiel 20:41 KJV)

The word "savour" means a spiritually pleasant fragrance.

Other scriptures like, "and, lo, I am with you always, even unto the end of the world. Amen" (Matthew 28:20 KJV) validate you and refute any claims that you are alone. You are not alone or all by yourself. Jesus said, "I will not leave you comfortless: I will come to you" (John 14:18 KJV). Scriptures, like this one in the book of Colossians, refute any claims that you are not complete in your single status. This scripture applies to any Christian believer:

> And ye are complete in him [Jesus], which is the head of all principality and power. (Colossians 2:10 KJV)

Who should be able to imply or try to tell you that you are not as happy as someone else when God has told you that your happiness is in your hope in him?

> Happy is he that hath the God of Jacob for his help, whose hope is in the Lord his God. (Psalm 146:5 KJV)

Singleness is not about being in solitary *confinement*. You are incredibly blessed to have the time, freedom, and opportunity to engage in solitary *refinement* (Jepson 1970).

You do not have to be ashamed of who you are in your divine calling. Years ago, in my beginners swimming class, we learned how to tread water. In ten feet of water, we practiced treading water—or keeping our head above the water—by moving our arms around and kicking our legs in a circular motion. Sometimes you may feel that you are "treading water" or fighting just to try to keep your head above the water of your trials and tribulations. Hold your head up! *Keep praying* and *walking*! God has promised, "When thou passest through the waters, I will be with thee; and through the rivers, they shall not overflow thee: when though *walkest* through the fire, thou shalt not be burned; neither shall the flame kindle upon thee" (Isaiah 43:2 KJV).

Your special calling is by God's *grace*. Boldly embrace your calling and rebuke all efforts that would attempt to bring it *disgrace*! The house is all yours in which to pray, "Better is a dry morsel, and quietness therewith, than an house full of sacrifices with strife" (Proverbs 17:1 KJV).

One of the many gospel Christian songs that is an inspiration to me at all times is "Hold to God's Unchanging Hand" (1906) by Jennie B. Wilson. This song is a real help in building one's courage, faith, and strength. Apostle Paul said, "But by the grace of God I am what I am: and his grace which was bestowed upon me was not in vain" (1 Corinthians 15:10 KJV). It is also good to know that neither is our labor in the Lord in vain (1 Corinthians 15:58).

All that has been said and expounded upon in this book is all by divine inspiration and direction. Like Jeremiah who was walking and operating in the office of a prophet, I had the leading of the Lord for this God-given assignment to write this book for this day and time.

> Thus speaketh the Lord God of Israel, saying, *Write* thee all the words that I have spoken unto thee in *a book*. (Jeremiah 30:2 KJV)

I thank God that I am *confirmed* by him (1 Corinthians 1:8 KJV). Through God's eyes, the people of God are seen as spiritual pottery, as the title and theme of this book describes.

> Though the precious people of Zion were like fine gold, how they are valued like the clay vessels, the handiwork of the potter. (Lamentations 4:2 ISV)

Apostle Paul further elaborated on this people-pottery connection and how God had a plan for us even before we were born when he said, "And that he might make known the riches of his glory on the *vessels* of mercy, which he had afore prepared unto glory" (Romans 9:23 KJV).

Keep being faithful, praying, staying encouraged, trusting God's word, and *hearing and saying* what God is saying about you, and don't deter from it!

> For we are his *workmanship*, created in Christ Jesus unto good works, which God hath before ordained that we should *walk* in them. (Ephesians 2:10 KJV)

If you have been given the gift of general prophecy (1 Corinthians 14:3, 5 NIV) or if you have been called into the *office of a prophet* (1 Corinthians 12:28 KJV and Ephesians 4:11–12 KJV), continue to press forward and walk in your prophetic calling. Boldly speak the messages that God gives to you and uphold that precious and special clay-human connection where we can let God shape, reshape, use, and lead us in every area of our lives!

Regarding those who have the gift of general prophecy or those called and operating in the office of a prophet, as it relates to the body of Christ, the scriptures say, "For as we have members in one body, and all members have not the same office" (Romans 12:4 KJV).

> But every man hath his proper gift of God, one after this manner, and another after that. (1 Corinthians 7:7 KJV)

Whatever your calling is, it is important to remember this important scriptural word of encouragement: "Cast not away therefore your confidence, which hath great recompence of reward" (Hebrews 10:35 KJV). On any matter of life, before you *decide*, let the Lord *guide*.

I hope that you have been blessed by reading my book. This book is a spiritually inspired and relevant literary reading experience. Some biblical perspectives, archaeology concepts, and visual images were explored in the context of ancient art, pottery, the clay-human connection, and walking victoriously through the trials and triumphs of a prophetic calling, especially those who are single as they walk in their divinely appointed journey with the Lord.

> Now thanks be unto God, which always causeth us to triumph in Christ, and maketh manifest the savour [pleasant fragrance] of his knowledge by us in every place. (2 Corinthians 2:14 KJV)

> Therefore, my brothers and sisters, make every effort to confirm your calling and election. For if you do these things, you will never stumble. (2 Peter 1:10 NIV)

The prophet Isaiah so vividly turned his spiritually inspired observation into this eloquently expressed proclamation: "How beautiful upon the mountains are the feet of him that bringeth good tidings, that *publisheth* peace; that bringeth good tidings of good, that *publisheth* salvation; that saith unto Zion, Thy God reigneth!" (Isaiah 52:7 KJV).

> Now unto him that is able to keep you from falling, and to present you faultless before the presence of his glory with exceeding joy, To the only wise God our Saviour, be glory and majesty, dominion and power, both now and ever. Amen. (Jude 24–25 KJV)

References

Abd-Allah, R., al-Muheisen, Z., and al-Howadi, S. 2010. Cleaning strategies of pottery objects excavated from Khirbet Edh-Dharih and Hayyan Al-Mushref, Jordan: Four case studies. *Mediterranean Archaeology and Archaeometry*, 10(2), 97–110.

Albertson, C. and Davidson, M. 2009. Drawing with Light and Clay: Teaching and Learning in the Art Studio as Pathways to Engagement. International *Journal of Education & Arts*, 8(9), 1–22. Retrieved from https://www.researchgate.net

Alisma, H. A., and McGuire, P. 2015. 21st Century Standards and Curriculum: Current Research and Practice. *Journal of Education and Practice*, 6(6), 150–151.

Allen, F. 2017. *Knowing and Living into Our Spiritual Gifts.* 1–75. Retrieved from https://www.stdavidchurch.org.

Alvermann, D. E., Gillis, V. R. and Phelps, S. F. 2013. *Content Area Reading and Literacy: Succeeding in Today's Diverse Classrooms* (7th ed.). Upper Saddle River, NJ: Pearson.

Archaeological Institute of America. 2016. The World's Oldest Writing. Retrieved from https://www.archaeolology.org.

Artson, B. S. 2009. Clay in the Potter's Hands: Human Evolution in a Self-Creating World. *Tikkun,* 24(1), 7–9.

Asbell, J. and Head, K. 2014. Jeremiah 18:1–12. Retrieved from https://www.nextsunday.com.

Ayee, E. S. A. 2013. Human Communication: A Biblical Perspective. *Bulletin for Christian Scholarship,* 78(1), 1–16.

Axelsen, M. and Arcodia, C. 2004. New Directions for Art Galleries and Museums: The Use of Special Events to Attract Audiences, a Case Study of the Asia Pacific Triennial. 1–16. Retrieved from https://www.espace.library.uq.edu.au.

Bader, T. 2017. How to Start Keeping a Prophetic Prayer Journal. Retrieved from https://www.timbaderonline.com.

Bae, Y. S. and Kim, D. H. 2018. The Applied Effectiveness of Clay Art Therapy for Patients with Parkinson's Disease. *Journal of Evidence-Based Integrative Medicine,* 23, 1–8.

Bandoim, L. 2015. The Benefits of Taking a Pottery Class for Children. Retrieved from https://www.blog.activityhero.com.

Bartel, M. 2006. Clay for Toddlers and Preschoolers: How and Why. Retrieved from bartelart.com.

———. 2016. How to Rework Clay & Fire without a Kiln. Retrieved from https://www.goshen.edu.

Biggam, S. and Itterly, K. 2009. *Literacy Profiles: A Framework to Guide Assessment, Instructional Strategies and Intervention, K-4,* NY: Allyn and Bacon.

Boehm, R. G., Hoone, C., McGowan, T. M., McKinney-Browning, M. C., Miramontes, O. B., and Porter, P. H. 2000. *Early United States.* Harcourt Brace Social Studies. San Francisco, CA: Harcourt Brace & Company.

Botwid, K. 2013. Evaluation of Ceramics: Professional Artisanship as a Tool for Archaeological Interpretation. *Journal of Nordic Archaeological Science,* 18, 31–44.

Boudreau, J. C. 1923. Clay as a Medium through which Educational Ideals May Be Effectively Presented. *Journal of the American Ceramic Society.* doi:10.1111/j.1151-2916.1923.tb19934.x.

Bradley, M. 2018. God Is no Respecter of Persons. Retrieved from https://www.bible-knowledge.com.

Breuer, S. 2012. The Chemistry of Pottery. Royal Society of Chemistry. Retrieved from https://www.edu.rsc.org.

Briggs, S. 2017. Genetics Has Proven that You're Unique—Just Like Everyone Else. Retrieved from https://www.qz.com.

Brighton, S. 2011. Applied Archeology and Community Collaboration: Uncovering the Past and Empowering the Present. *Human Organization: Journal of the Society for Applied Anthropology,* 70(4), 344–354.

Brinck, I. and Reddy, V. 2019. Dialogue in Making: Emotional Engagement with Materials. *Phenomenology and the Cognitive Sciences,* 19, 23–45.

Bristol, T. and Isaac, E. P. 2009. Christian Education and Constructivism: Learning through the Adult Sunday School Class. Adult Education Research Conference.

Budiselic, E. 2014. The Old Testament Concept of Revival within the New Testament. KAROS-*Evangelistic Journal of Theology,* 8(1), 45–74.

Burrison, J. 2017. International Folk Pottery: A Brief Primer. In *Global Clay: Themes in World Ceramic Traditions* (pp. 10–35). Bloomington, IN: Indiana University Press.

Bustamante, A. S., Greenfield, D. B., and Nayfeld, I. 2018. Early Childhood Science and Engineering: Engaging Platforms for Fostering Domain General Learning Skills. *Education Sciences,* 8(3),1–13.

Butterfield, K. 2018. Favoritism in the Church. Retrieved from https://www.tabletalkmagazine.com.

Buyer, P. 2013. 10 Tips to Becoming a Better Writer. Retrieved from https://www.paulbuyer.com.

Cantrell, R. 2001. You Are the Potter: I Am the Clay. Israel Touching Letter. *Bridges for Peace. Your Israel Connection,* 77901, 1–6.

Capella 2008. *Ancient history: Explore the Past.* London, England: Arctures Publishing Limited.

Caram, P. G. 2010. *Turning the Curse into a Blessing.* Teachers Manual. Ulysses, PA: Zion Christian Publications.

Carlo, R. 2017. Getting Centered: A Meditation on Creating Pottery and Teaching Writing. *Journal of the Assembly for Expanded Perspectives on Learning (JAEPL)* 22, 92–102.

Carma, H. 2017. Major and Minor Prophets Were of Equal Importance. Westgate Gazette. Retrieved from https://www.thewestsidegazette.com.

Carr, K. E. 2017. History of Pottery: Clay Pottery. Quatr.us Study Guides. Retrieved from https://www.quatr.us.

Carretero, M. I. 2002. Clay Minerals and Their Beneficial Effect upon Human Health. *Applied Clay Science,* 21, 155–163.

Carrigan, L. 2019. The American Art Pottery Association: Why You Should Join. Arts and Crafts Collector. Retrieved from https://www.artsandcraftscollector.com.

Cauley, K. M. and Milan, J. H. 2010. Formative Assessment Techniques to Support Student Motivation and Achievement. *The Clearing House,* 83(1), 1–6.

Chinn-Lee, C. and Pena, T. 1999. *A-Is for the Americas.* New York, NY: Orchard Books.

Choi, C. Q. 2008. Ancient Mayans: Temples for Everyone! Retrieved from https://www.livescience.com.

Clark, I. 2008. Assessment Is for Learning: Formative Assessment and Positive Learning Interactions. *Florida Journal of Educational Administration & Policy,* 2(1), 1–16.

———. 2015. Formative Assessment: Translating High-Level Curriculum Principles into Classroom Practice. *The Curriculum Journal,* 26(1), 91–114.

Clark, N. A., Heflin, T., Kluball, J., and Kramer, E. 2015. Understanding Music: Past and Present. Galileo Open Learning Materials. Retrieved from https://www.oer.galileo.usg.edu.

Clarke, A. 2019. What Is Prophesy and the Prophetic?: Here's Everything You Want to Know. Retrieved from https://www.catchthefire.com.

Corazzo, J. 2019. Materialising the Studio: A Systematic Review of the Material Space of the Studio in Art, Design and Architecture. *The Design Journal,* 22(1), 1249–1265.

Crown, P. L. 2014. The Archaeology of Crafts Learning: Becoming a Potter in the Puebloan Southwest. *Annual Review of Anthropology,* 43, 71–88.

Dalile, B. 2015. Kintsukuroi: Suffering and Love. Retrieved from https://www.medium.com.

Danien, E. C. 2006. Paintings of Maya Pottery: The Art and Career of M. Louise Baker. Retrieved from https://www.famsi.org.

Dein, S. and Cook, C. H. 2014. God Put a Thought in My Mind: The Charismatic Christian Experience of Receiving Communications from God. *Mental Health, Religion, & Culture,* 18(2), 97–113.

DiNardi, G. 2019. Why You Should Work Less and Spend More Time on Hobbies. Harvard Business Review. Retrieved from https://www.hbr.org.

Djamil, B. 2016. Sun-Dried Clay for Sustainable Constructions. *International Journal of Applied Engineering Research,* 11(6), 4628–4633.

Drew, W. F., Christie, J., Johnson, J. E., Meckley, A. M., and Neil, M. L. 2008. Constructive Play: A Value-Added Strategy for Meeting Early Learning Standards. *Young Children,* 63(4), 38–44.

Elbrecht, C. and Antcliff, C. R. 2014. Being Touched Through Touch: Trauma Treatment through Haptic Perception at the Clay Field: A Sensorimotor Art Therapy. *International Journal of Art Therapy,* 19(1), 19–30.

Ellison, R. 1984. The Uses of Pottery. *Iraq,* 46(1), 63–68. doi:10.2307/4200212.

Erickson, T. 2015. Molding the Future: Child Development through Work with Clay. Retrieved from https://www.bingschool.stanford.edu.

Ezrachimts 2016. Lessons Learned from the Potter: Jeremiah 18:1–6. Flaming the Fire of Christ. Retrieved from https://www.ezrachimts.wordpress.com.

Fairchild, M. 2019. Major and Minor Prophetic Books of the Bible. Retrieved from https://www.learnreligions.com.

Fan, P. 2017. The Transmission of Symbolic Meaning in Modern Ceramic Product Design. *Advances in Economics, Business and Management Research (AEBMR),* 14, 107–109.

Fayt, D. 2020. Pottery Careers: Expert Insights into Making a Living as a Potter. Ceramic Arts Network. Retrieved from https://www.ceramicartsnetwork.org.

Feen-Calligan, H., Moreno, J., and Buzzard, 2018. Art Therapy, Community Building, Activism, and Outcomes. *Frontiers in Psychology,* 9(1548), 1–17.

Fenenga, G. L., Erwin, B., and Erwin, W. 2015. A Prehistoric Ceramic Rattle from the Southwestern Shoreline of Ancient Lake Cahuilla, Imperial County, California. *Pacific Coast Archaeological Society Quarterly,* 51(1).

Ferrari, M., Bouffard, T., and Rainville, L. 1998. What Makes a Good Writer?: Differences in Good and Poor Writers' Self-Regulation of Writing. *Instructional Science,* 26, 473–488.

Foley, N. K. 2009. Environmental Characteristics of Clays and Clay Mineral Deposits. The U.S. Geological Survey (USGS). Retrieved from https://www.pubs.usgs.gov.

Freeman-Ellis, V. 1989. *First Book of Africa: An Introduction for Young Readers.* Orange, NJ: Just Us Books, Inc.

Friedel, R. 2010. Materials that Changed History. Retrieved from https://www.pbs.org.

Garcia, L.L. 2018. The Mayan Gods: An Explanation from the Structures of Thought. *Journal of Historical Archaeology & Anthropological Sciences,* 3(1), 96–112.

Genoe, M. R. and Liechty, T. 2017. Meanings of Participation in a Leisure Arts Pottery Program. *World Leisure Journal,* 59, 91–104.

Godwin, R. 2019. Throws of Passion: How Pottery Became a Refuge from our Hyperconnected Times. The Guardian. Retrieved from https://www.the guardian.com.

Gordon, A. R. 1903. A Study of Jeremiah. II. *The Biblical World,* 22(3), 195–208.

Grace House. 2015. The Revival Meeting. Retrieved from https://www.gracehouseclinton.com.

Griffiths, D. 1999. The Role of Interdisciplinary Science in the Study of Ancient Pottery. *Interdisciplinary Science Reviews,* 24(4), 289–300.

Gulley, D. 2016. "Where He Leads Me, I Will Follow." Retrieved from https://www.lordletmegrow.com.

Hall, B. 2006. *From Mud to Music.* Columbus, OH: American Ceramic Society.

Hawn, C. M. 2013. History of hymns. "Have Thine Own Way, Lord." Retrieved from https://www.umcdiscipleship.org.

Haywood, A. 2021. *Take Up Your Bed and Walk: This Is My Story!* Meadville, PA: Christian Faith Publishing, Inc.

Health Fitness Revolution. 2019. Top 10 Health Benefits of Pottery. Retrieved from https://www.healthfitnessrevolution.com.

High, B. 2019. The Surprising Legacy of Jeremiah, the Prophet. Retrieved from https://www.billhigh.com.

Hirst, K. K. 2018. An Introduction to Seriation: Scientific Dating Before Radiocarbon. Retrieved from https://www.thoughtco.com.

Hocine, Z., Zhang, J., Song, Y., and Ye, L. 2014. Autonomy-Supportive Leadership Behavior Contents. *Open Journal of Social Sciences, 2,* 433-.

Hoffeditz, D. M. 2015. They Were Single, Too: A Sampling of 8 Bible Characters. Retrieved from https:www.voice.dts.edu.

Hogeterp, A. 2018. Prophesy and the Prophetic as Aspects of Paul's theology. *Stellenbosch Theological Journal,* 4(2), 169–196.

Houston, S. D. 1999. Classic Maya Religion: Beliefs and Practices of an Ancient American People. *Brigham Young University Studies,* 38(4), 43–72.

Humphries, T. 2017. Pottery for Beginners: Equipment & Tools Needed to get Started. Retrieved from https://www.thelittlepotcompany.co.uk.

Hyatt, J. P. 2020. Jeremiah. Encyclopedia Britannica. Retrieved from https://www.britannica.com.

Hymnary. 2007. *My Hope Is Built on Nothing Less.* Retrieved from https://www.hymnary.org.

Im, D. 2017. Broken Vessels. Retrieved from https://danielim.com.

Ion, R. M., Fierascu, R. C., Teodorescu, S., Fierascu, I., Bunghez, I. R., Turcanu-Carutiu, D., and Ion, M.L. 2016. Ceramic

Materials Based on Clay Materials in Cultural Heritage Study. doi:10.5772/61633.

Irekamba, C. 2015. Why Do Envy, Jealousy Exist in God's House? The Guardian Nigeria News. Retrieved from https://www.guardian.ng.

Jacobs, C. 1995. *The Voice of God.* Ventura, CA: Regal Books. Retrieved from https://www.irp-cdn.multiscreensite.com.

James, F. W. 1962. The Pottery of the Old Testament. *Expedition Magazine,* 5(1), 1–14.

Jang, H. and Choi, S. 2012. Increasing Ego-Resilience Using Clay with Low SES (Social Economic Status) Adolescents in Group Art Therapy. *The Arts in Psychotherapy,* 39, 245–250.

Jepson, S. 1970. *For the Love of Singles.* Carol Stream, IL: Creation House.

Jones, T. P. 2018. Prophets, Priests, and Kings Today?: Theological and Practical Problems with the Use of the Munus Triplex as a Leadership Topology. *Perichoresis,* 16(3), 63–86.

Joyce, R. A., Hendon, J. A., and Lopiparo, J. 2014. Working with Clay. *Ancient Mesoamerica,* 25(2), 411–420.

Kabanda, P. 2015. Work as Art: Links between Creative Work and Human Development. Human Development Report Office. 1–28. Retrieved from https://www.hdr.undp.org.

Karim, S. K. and Amin, O. S. M. 2018. Stroke in Ancient Mesopotamia. *Medical Archives(Sarajevo, Bosnia, and Herzegovina),* 72(6), 449–452.

Kiger, P. J. 2019. 9 Ancient Sumerian Inventions that Changed the World. Retrieved from https://www.history.com.

Kimport, E. R. and Robbins, S. J. 2012. Efficacy of Creative Clay Work for Reducing Negative Mood: A Randomized Controlled Trial. *Art Therapy,* 29(2).

Konta, J. 1995. Clay and Man: Clay Raw Materials in the Service of Man. *Applied Clay Science,* 10(4), 275–335.

Kourkouta, L., Koukourikos, K., Iliadis, C., Ouzounakis, P., Monios, A., and Tsaloglidou, A. 2017. Bread and Health. *Journal of Pharmacy and Pharmacology,* 5, 821–826.

Kranz, J. 2014. Jeremiah: Jerusalem's Rebellion, Punishment, and Hope. Retrieved from https:www.overviewbible.com.

Kurz, E. 2017. Why Is Historical Context Important when Studying God's Word? Ethnos360 Bible Institute. Retrieved from https://www.369bible.org.

Laal, M. and Salamati, P. 2012. Lifelong Learning: Why Do We Need It? *Social and Behavioral Sciences,* 31, 399–403.

LeClaire, J. 2014. Are You Called as a Prophet?: Here Are 2 Ways to Know. Retrieved from https://www.charismanews.com.

LeCount, C. J. 2018. Lessons Learned in Seriating Maya Pottery. *Engaging Archaeology: 25 Case Studies in Research Practice.* doi.org/10.1002/9781119240549.ch21.

Lloyd, K. 2017. Benefits of Art Education: A Review of the Literature. *Scholarship and Engagement in Education,* 1(1).

Lunenburg, F. C. 2011. Early Childhood Education: Implications for School Readiness. *Schooling,* 2(1),1–8.

Lusebrink, V. B. 2004. Art Therapy and the Brain: An Attempt to Understand the Underlying Processes of Art Expression in Therapy. *Art Therapy: Journal of the American Art Therapy Association,* 21(3), 125–135.

Lynch, V. and Hancock, C. 2012. Solving Crime with DNA. *Quest,* 8(2), 3–9.

Mana, S. C. A., Hanafiah, M. M., and Chowdhury, A. J. K. 2017. Environmental Characteristics of Clay and Clay-Based Materials. *Geology, Ecology, and Landscapes,* 1(3), 155–161.

Manoharan, C., Sutharsan, P., Dhanapandian, S., and Venkatachalapathy, R. 2012. Characteristics of Some Clay Materials from Tamilnadu, India, and Their Possible Ceramic Uses. *Ceramica,* 59, 412–418.

Marchetti, C. 2018. Women Prophets in the Old Testament. *Pricilla Papers, 32*(2), 9-13.

Margalit, A. 2018. Jeremiah's Autonomy: The Book of Jeremiah. *Social Research: An International Quarterly,* 85(3), 627–637.

Mark, J. J. 2014. Daily Life in Mesopotamia. Retrieved from https://www.ancient.eu.

———. 2011. Writing: Definition. Ancient History Encyclopedia. Retrieved from https://www.ancient.eu.

Marovich, B. 2012. Hold to God's Unchanging Hand—Eric Carrington. Retrieved from journalofgospelmusic.com.

Mart, C. T. 2019. Reader-Response Theory and Literature Discussions: A Springboard for Exploring Literacy Texts. *Then New Educational Review*, 78–87. doi:10.15804/tner.2019.56.2.06.

Martikainen, J. 2017. Making Pictures as a Method of Teaching Art History. *International Journal of Education & the Arts*, 18(19), 1–24.

Martin, E. L. 1999. Introduction to Jeremiah. Associates for Scriptural Knowledge. Retrieved from https://www.askelm.com.

Martin, J., Obille, V. P., Apigo, M. A., Gongora, A. C., Labsan, J., Navalta, M. E., and Oringo, F. 2016. Historical Background of the Pottery Industry in Taboe, San Juan, La Union. De La Salle University Research Congress, Manila, Philippines. Retrieved from https://www.disu.edu.ph/.

McConville, J. G. 1991. Jeremiah: Prophet and Book. *Tyndale Bulletin*, 47, (1), 80–95.

McIntosh, M. A. 2017. Art History: Thinking and Talking about Art. Retrieved from https://www.brewminate.com.

McLeod, S. 2019. Social Identity Theory. Simply Psychology. Retrieved from https://www.simplypsychology.org.

Minnesota Historical Society. 1–6. Retrieved from https:www.muhs.org.

Minnicks, M. 2020. Singleness: What the Bible Says about Being Single. Retrieved from https://www.pairedlife.com.

Minnix, J. M. 2005. Seven Steps to an Effective Revival. Georgia Baptist Convention. Retrieved from https://www.sermons.pastorlife.com.

Mitchell, S. 2018. Master Potter Encourages Students to Refine Craft. The Harvard Gazette. Retrieved from https://www.news.harvard.edu

Mugurussa, T. 2012. Learning with Play Dough. Retrieved from https://www.scholastic.com.

Mullins, R.1988. "Awesome God." BMG Music, Inc. Retrieved from https://www.hymnary.org.

Mustard, J. F. 2010. Early Brain Development and Development. Retrieved from https://www.childhood-encyclopedia.com.

Nan, J. K. M. and Ho, R. T. H. 2017. Effects of Clay Art Therapy on Adults Outpatients with Major Depressive Disorder: A Randomized Controlled Trial. *Journal of Affective Disorders*, 217, 237–245.

Nelson, K. 2005. *He's Got the Whole World in His Hands*. New York, NY: Dial.

Nespeca, S. M. 2012. The Importance of Play, Particularly Constructive Play in Public Library Programming. A White Paper Written for the Association for Library Services to Children. Retrieved from https://www.ala.org.

Nicholson, P. T. 2009. Pottery Production. *UCLA Encyclopedia of Egyptology*, 1(1), 1–8.

Noice, T., Noice, H., and Kramer, A. F. 2014. Participatory Arts for Older Adults: A Review of Benefits and Challenges. *Gerontologist*, 54(5), 741–753.

Nordquist, R. 2020. Definition and Examples of Context Clues. Retrieved from https://www.thoughtco.com.

O'Hagan, A. and Calder, R. 2020. DNA and Fingerprint Recovery from an Arson Scene. *Forensic Research & Criminology International Journal*, 8(1), 15–29.

Otto, F. 2016. Study: Just 45 Minutes of Art-Making Improves Self-Confidence. Arts & Culture, Health & Medicine. Retrieved from https://www.newsblog.drexel.edu.

Ovidiu-Iliuta, D. 2013. Employee Motivation and Organizational Performance. *Review of Applied Socio-Economic Research*, 5(1), 53–60.

Owens, J. J. 1981. Jeremiah, Prophet of True Religion. *Review & Expositor*, 78(3), 365–379.

Pang, K. 2009. An Examination of Constructivist-Driven Instructional Design and Its Pedagogical Implications for Effective Learning. *Transformative Dialogues: Teaching & Learning Journal,* 3(2),1–9.

Peace, K. L. and Pruss, A. B. 2012. Understanding Omnipotence. *Religious Studies,* 48, 403–414.

Peacock, D. P. S. 1970. The Scientific Analysis of Ancient Ceramics: A Review. *World Archaeology,* 1(3), 375–389.

Peckham, J. C. 2007. The Passible Potter and the Contingent Clay: A Theological Study of Jeremiah 18:1–10. *Journal of the Adventist Theological Society,* 18(1), 130–150.

Peterson, B. 2019. The Difference between Pottery and Ceramics. The Space Crafts. Retrieved from https://www.thesprucecrafts.com.

Pope, C. 2018. Who Was Jeremiah the Prophet? Retrieved from https://www.blog.adw.org.

Queiroz, R. 2018. Individual Liberty and the Importance of the Concept of the People. Palgrave Communications. Retrieved from https://www.nature.com.

Rainer, T.S. 2014. Fourteen Symptoms of Toxic Church Leaders. Retrieved from https://www.churchanswers.com.

Ranson, A. 2019. The Benefits of Playing with Play Dough. Retrieved from https://www.theimaginationtree.com.

Reddit, P. L. 2008. *Introduction to the Prophets.* Queenswood, South Africa: Eerdmans Publishing.

Richman-Abdou, K. 2019. Kintsugi: The Centuries-Old Art of Repairing Broken Pottery with Gold. Retrieved from https://www.mymodernmet.com.

Righi, D., & Meunier, A. 1995. *Origin and Mineralogy of Clays: Clays and the Environment.* Berlin, Germany: Springer-Verlag Berlin Heidelberg.

Roberts, J. R. 2013. Biblical Cosmology: The Implications for Bible Translation. *Journal of Translation,* 9(2), 1–53.

Romig, J. M. 2019. Everyday Wisdom: The Benefits of Wisdom. Retrieved from https://www.cornerstonewestford.com.

Sanders, A. 2012. Rosenblatt's Presence in the New Literacies Research. *National Conference of Teachers of English*, 24(1), 1–6.

Savelle, J. 1998. *From Devastation to Restoration: The Secret to Recovering from Life's Most Devastating Experiences.* Crowley, TX: Jerry Savelle Publications. Retrieved from https:www.static1.squarespace.com.

Sawchuk, E. and Prendergast, M. 2019. Archaeological Discoveries Are Happening Faster than Ever Before, Helping Refine the Human Story. Retrieved from https://www.theconversation.com.

Schmandt-Besserat, D. 1977. The Earliest Uses of Clay in Syria. Penn Museum. *Expedition Magazine,* 19(3).

Sessions, B. 1997. A New Case for Clay: Multi-Dimensional High School Ceramics. *Marilyn Zurmuehlin Working Papers in Art Education,* 14, 93–106.

Sharp, T. 2017. Periodic Table of the Elements. Retrieved from https://www.livescience.com.

Sheehan, G. 2020. Digging Clay by Hand: How to Process Clay from the Ground. Ceramic Arts Network. Retrieved from https://www.ceramicartsnetwork.org.

Sholt, M. and Gavron, T. 2006. Therapeutic Qualities of Clay-Work in Art Therapy and Psychotherapy: A review. *Art Therapy Journal of the American Art Therapy Association,* 23(2), 66–72.

Short, K. G., Lynch-Brown, C. M., and Tomlinson, C. M. 2014. *Essentials of Children's Literature* (8th ed.). Upper Saddle River, NJ: Pearson.

Simundson, D. J. 2002. Preaching from Jeremiah: Challenges and Opportunities. *Word & World,* 22(4), 423–432.

Skibo, J. and Feinman, G. 1999. *Pottery and People.* Salt Lake, UT: University of Utah Press.

Smith, F. 2012. Marriage—Good or Bad? Retrieved from https://www.answersingenesis.org.

Smith, G. T. 2009. *Courage and Calling: Embracing Your God-given Potential.* Westmont, IL: InterVarsity Press.

Smith, R. H. 2014. What Is the Difference between Envy and Jealousy? Retrieved from https://www.psychologytoday.co.

Solheim, O. H. 2018. What Is Good Writing?: What Is a Good Reading Experience? Retrieved From https://www.writingcooperative.com.

Spencer, N. 2003. *The British Museum of Egyptian Hieroglyphs.* London, England: Barnes & Noble, Inc.

Stancil, D. C. 2013. The Major Prophets. Retrieved from https://www.dcstancil.com.

Staubach, S. 2005. *Clay: The History and Evolution of Humankind's Relationship with Earth's Most Primal Element.* Ann Arbor, MI: Berkley Books.

Straiton, J. 2018. Not-So-Identical Twins. Retrieved from https://www.biotechniques.com.

Sussman, K. S. 2012. The Importance of Play in the Preschool Classroom. *Texas Childcare Quarterly,* 36(3), 1–8.

Sutakova, E. and Mestnikov, A. 2018. Basics of Recreation of Ancient Ceramics Production Technology. *MATEC Web Conferences,* 143, 1–6. Retrieved from https://www.matec-conferences.org.

Swartz, M.I. 2005. Playdough: What's Standard About it? *Young Children,* 60(2), 100–109. The Holy Bible. 1984. In the King James Version. Thomas Nelson Publishers.

Terreni, L. 2015. Using Clay to Scaffold and Understand Children's Expressions. Retrieved from https://www.earlyarts.uk.

Thompson, D. and Miller-Perrin, C. 2003. Understanding Vocation: Discerning and Responding to God's call. *Leven,* 11(1), 1–6.

Thompson, J. A. 2010. What Is Your Calling? Retrieved from https://www.speeches.byu.edu.

M. S. 2008. Ceramic Production, Provenance and Use: A review. *Archaeometry,* 50(2), 216–231.

Tranquillo, J. 2008. Kinesthetic Learning in the Classroom. *American Society for Engineering Education,* 1–9.

Tsetlin, Y. 2018. The Origin of Ancient Pottery Production. *Journal of Historical Archaeology & Anthropological Sciences,* 3(2), 193–198.

Uchida, E. and Watanabe, R. 2014. Blackening of Surfaces of Mesopotamian Clay Tablets Due to Manganese Precipitation. *Archaeological Discovery*, 2, 107–116.

Vasu, C. 2011. What's in a Clay?: Finding the Right Minerals for Salt Glaze Pottery. Retrieved from https://www.kque.org.

Vellet, M. G. 2014. *Art Therapy as an Instrument of Peace,* pp. 112-142*: Clay Art and Dance as Instruments of Peace and Social Justice.* Retrieved from https://www.researchgate.net.

Vincentelli, M. 2000. *Women and Ceramics: Gendered Vessels (Studies in design).* Manchester, UK: Manchester University Press.

Violatti, C. 2014. Pottery in Antiquity. *Ancient History Encyclopedia.* Retrieved from https://www.ancient.eu/pottery/.

Walton, J. 2017. Kintsugi and Our God of Restoration. Retrieved from https://www.mendedlife.com.

Weier, K. 2004. Empowering Young Children in Art Museums: Letting Them Take the Lead. *Contemporary Issues in Early Childhood,* 1(1), 106–116.

West, D. 2018. A Step-By-Step Guide for Creating Clay Rattles. Retrieved from https://www.theartofeducation.edu.

Westrup, J. A. and Grame, T. C. 2019. Musical Instrument. Encyclopedia Britannica, Inc. Retrieved from https://www.britannica.com.

Williams, L. B. and Haydel, S. E. 2010. Evaluation of the Medicinal Use of Clay Minerals as Antibacterial Agents. *International Geology Review,* 52(718), 745–770.

Wong, X. C. and Benson, K. 2019. A Guided Exploration-Based Visual Arts Program for Preschoolers. NAEYC. *Young Children,* 74(1).

Woodford, C. 2019. Ceramics. Retrieved from https://www.explainthisstuff.com.

Woods, L. 2014. Prophets and the Prophetic Call. *Echoing the Word,* 3, 1–3. Retrieved from

Youngblood, R. 1990. The Call of Jeremiah. *Criswell Theological Review,* 5(1), 99–108.

CPSIA information can be obtained
at www.ICGtesting.com
Printed in the USA
JSHW060008020722
27723JS00005B/135